To Cindy:
My partner in struggles, in joys,
and in experiencing the fullness of life
given to us by Jesus.

Struggle Well

Living through Life's Storms

Michael W. Newman

STRUGGLE WELL
Published by CreateSpace Publishing
A division of Amazon.com

©2010 Michael W. Newman

Printed in the United States of America

For information:
www.mnewman.org

•

Contents

Chapter One
Struggle Well

"And now my life ebbs away; days of suffering grip me...The churning inside me never stops; days of suffering confront me."
Job 30:16, 27

"The LORD said, 'I have indeed seen the misery of my people in Egypt. I have heard them crying out because of their slave drivers, and I am concerned about their suffering.'" Exodus 3:7

The Deep Ache

I didn't want to get out of bed. I didn't want to face the day. Honestly, I didn't know if I could. To be totally honest, I didn't care if I lived anymore. For some reason, darkness had enveloped me. I had big questions about my purpose in life. How did I fit? Where did I belong? What was God's plan for me? Would these feelings of pain and displacement stop? Would I ever emerge from this dark night of the soul? I read the words of Psalm 102:9-10 and felt like the writer was talking about my life: *"I eat ashes as my food and mingle my drink with tears because of your great wrath, for you have taken me up and thrown me aside."* I felt as if God had thrown me aside, that I was in limbo, not much use to Him or anyone. I was struggling.

That is what this book is about. Struggle. Trouble. Suffering. Hurt. Trial. Testing. Sometimes struggles hit with sudden impact. Crisis, illness, tragedy, and grief rise up quickly and surprise you with a tidal wave of deep and overwhelming pain. A test of your character springs up in front of you. It's a do or die moment. Will you or won't you? The path of least resistance or the road less traveled? At other times, a slow accumulation of difficulties, mishaps, setbacks, disappointments, and heartbreaks gather in the depths of your mind and soul. Subtly, quietly, the clouds of despair gather and a season of darkness sets in. Gradually you slide into depression or addiction or bitterness or anger.

My deep ache formed gradually. I'm not certain of all of the ingredients of the recipe that formed my struggle, but the concoction of pain was helped along by a few key events in life. First, I experienced a major disappointment when I was not chosen for a ministry position. I thought God was directing me to it. Everything and everyone appeared to be lined up perfectly for the new and exciting next step. The timing seemed ideal. But it didn't happen. I wasn't chosen. Shortly after the decision was made, I saw that it would have been a disaster to be thrown into that situation. But I was still disappointed and confused. My equilibrium had been tossed out of balance.

During this time, my wife and I had also entered into a new season of parenting. High School began for my children. With it came a new attitude toward mom and dad. Gone was the sweet loyalty of grade school. The free affection of childhood and the easy smiles of innocent youth waned. Trust for mom and dad became a thing of the past. Even the ability to be involved as a room parent or field trip chaperone was eliminated in the new high school scenario. Family, once a refuge from the turbulence of life, now became another struggle. Where there was once peace, there was conflict. Where there was once delight, there was difficulty. The years marched forward and the challenges became more and more intense.

During this span of time, I also experienced the death of many dear people. As a pastor, funerals are a staple of life. But after serving in a congregation for more than a decade, the people were not strangers. They were friends, loved ones. Their hurt caused hurt in me. Their losses were my losses. Unfortunately, when you are comforting the grieving, you sometimes miss out on your own grief process. Over a period of ten months, sixteen people died. One was my grandmother. Two were babies. Several were precious friends. The accumulation of grief was tiring and very sad.

In the midst of these struggles, we made the decision to change ministries. This involved a move across the country. As a family, we were in agreement that it was God's plan and calling. All of us were excited about the change. But it wasn't easy. We left the home where our children had grown up. We left a church that I had grown with—an extended family for all of us. We left an area of the country where all the grandparents lived. We moved from familiar places and traditions to a new and foreign land— Texas! The people there were wonderful. We were happy with our home. The new opportunities were fantastic. But the turbulence created by such a radical change shook each of us more deeply than we realized.

Added to the mix was a running injury that would not heal. I love to run. I've been at it for many years. It's a part of my life that allows me to get outside, breathe fresh air, and see the beauty of God's creation. My running time is my praying time, my thinking time, and my soul therapy. Running keeps me physically and mentally healthy. It's a release. But a severe hip injury kept me from it for longer than I had ever been sidelined. I wondered if I would ever be able to run again. Had my age caught up with me? Was this the end? In addition to the worries about my running future, my body was in withdrawal from the intense regular exercise and the free flow of endorphins. Even though I exercised in other ways, nine months of wintery recovery gripped me.

With all the changes in my life and ministry, I also began to question what God really wanted me to do. In my previous congregation I was in a leadership role. Now I adjusted to a support position. Before, I was free to move ahead creatively. Now, I had to navigate obstacles and seek permission. Previously, I unleashed all my gifts and passion. Now, I had to hold back and pick and choose a few things to do. It was a confusing time.

Then came the Lariam. About seven months before the major ministry disappointment, my family and I went on a mission trip to West Africa. Part of the preparation for the journey involved taking some anti-malarial medicine. The drug Lariam was prescribed for me, my wife and my middle-school aged daughters. We dutifully took our doses for a few weeks before the trip, during our stay there, and for a few weeks after we returned home. Toward the end of the medication regimen we began to develop curious side effects. One of my daughters became unusually emotional at odd times. My other daughter struggled

10

with her homework. She couldn't put thoughts together. My wife and I started to forget things. I stood at a McDonald's restaurant, trying to give the cashier exact change, but I couldn't remember what coins added up to thirty-five cents. My wife forgot how to drive from school to home after she picked up our daughters at the end of the school day. I got lost on a run one morning—in my own neighborhood! Finally, the medication was finished and the symptoms were gone, but after reading about some very severe and dangerous effects of Lariam, I wondered how long the poison lingered in our systems. Could the long-term effects throw me into a valley of despair?

And so, I struggled. On every front of life I experienced the deep ache of darkness. I wasn't trying to figure out the cause. Only looking back do I see what might have contributed to the oppressive fog that enveloped me. I was simply living through it. I was slogging my way through change and challenge. I felt terrible, lousy, depressed, and sad. Not on the outside. I was pretty good at hiding the pain. I stuck with it and kept going. But inside I felt as if I could collapse at any moment. Inside I was crumbling. Inside I was crying. It went on for nearly eight years.

That's when God threw me a lifeline.

A Lifeline

I was visiting a church one Sunday. During these days of struggle, I was starving for morsels of hope, sips of some refreshment for my soul. As I listened to the pastor preach, he referenced Psalm 37. I looked up the Psalm in the Bible on my phone. This Bible happened to be an initial edition of the New Living Translation. The first verse that caught my ear was verse seven, *"Be still in the presence of the Lord, and wait patiently for him to act."* I was in a time of waiting. I knew I had to be patient during this season in the wilderness. Verse five of the Psalm told me I could trust God: *"Commit everything you do to the Lord. Trust him, and he will help you."* I needed His help. I had to trust that God was still alive, well, and working. The preacher skipped ahead a few verses to verse thirty-four. *"Don't be impatient for the Lord to act! Travel steadily along his path."* The verse exploded into my mind. What do I need to do during this time of waiting? What was my calling as I questioned, wrestled and struggled? It was to travel steadily along God's path.

This was huge for me. We'll talk about it in more detail in chapter three, but this verse became the moment by moment lifeline for my struggle. My calling during this time of darkness was not to hurry God. It was not to try to take His job. It was not to force the issue or to coerce Him into hastening His plan. I didn't want a life like that. Abraham and Sarah tried that. After waiting years for God's promised child with no result, Abraham and Sarah tried their own plan by having Abraham father a child through their servant, Hagar. Ishmael was born and trouble ensued.

> *This was huge for me…This verse became the moment by moment lifeline for my struggle.*

No, I didn't want an Ishmael life. I wanted an Isaac life—the promise, God's doing. My job was not to make things happen. It was to travel steadily along God's path. From moment to moment, from breath to breath, from heartbeat to heartbeat, from decision to decision, and from action to action, my job was to travel steadily and faithfully, bowing before God, trusting that He had a plan.

This was not easy, but it provided me with direction and a focus. In other words, in the midst of struggle I had a choice. I could struggle poorly. I could rage against God and everyone else. I could go off the deep end in disobedience and self-indulgence. I could throw a life-tantrum and chase after what would make me feel satisfied for the moment. I could despair and end it all.

Or, I could take another path. I could struggle well. I could trust God, wrestle with Him, wait on Him, talk to Him, be quiet and still with Him, accept His plan, and serve Him and the people around me. In the midst of my struggle, I could travel steadily along His path. I could struggle well.

That is how this book was born. Each one of us will encounter difficult struggles in life. Is there a godly way to live when those struggles hit? Is there a better course of action when hurt, depression, and the clouds of gloom saturate your life? We need to ask those questions because each one of us will be tested by darkness and despair. Each one of us will face storms.

Storms Will Come

Yes, storms will come. I have to admit that I'm a weather buff. I really love the weather. Not the weather outside, particularly. I love weather forecasts—meteorology! Weather forecasts have become extremely accessible these days. We all know how to talk about the weather. We know about high and low pressure systems. We are familiar with barometric pressure and the jet stream. We talk about El Niño and La Niña. Isobars, frontal systems, wind chills, the heat index, and dew points have become part of our vocabulary. I believe one of the greatest developments in the modern era is The Weather Channel! All weather, all the time—combined with smooth jazz. Can you think of anything better than that?

Okay, maybe I'm going overboard, but there is value in paying attention to weather forecasts. When warm air and cold air collide, you know a storm will form. You also know that weather systems are constantly on the move. One front may pass, but another one is always on the way. It may be a strong Nor'easter or an Alberta Clipper. Fronts from the south may bring moisture into the midsection of the country. The weather teaches you an important life principle: storms pass, but storms will come. Storms will always come.

Jesus' disciples discovered that principle as they were rowing across the Sea of Galilee. John chapter 6 tells us that Jesus was praying on a mountainside while His followers made their way across this body of water. Suddenly, as verse eighteen tells us, *"a gale swept down upon them."* This was not an unusual occurrence on the Sea of Galilee. Fierce storms came out of nowhere and swept fishermen to their deaths. The sea was known for these storms. In fact, during that time people called the Sea of Galilee "The Abyss" because of all the watery deaths that occurred there. So the disciples found themselves in the middle of a raging storm. The original Greek text says that the sea *"rose up"*—like the resurrection of a living being—to crush the disciples as they tried to row through the storm.

Storms will come—fierce, threatening, difficult, and hurtful. Storms will rise up in your life. They can paralyze you. Like icy blasts they can stop you in your tracks. Storms can blind

14

you. Like the thick winter winds filled with snow or like hurricane force winds laced with water, storms in your life can make you believe that no future lies ahead. You wish you knew when God would come through or when the pain would end, but all you can see is the difficult and distressing present. Storms can bring shock and destruction. As a bolt of lightning explodes on the earth, trial can explode into your life and create havoc. As a tornado tears apart everything in its path, struggles can destroy your hopes and dreams. Yes, storms will come.

This is not about the weather. It's about your life. Loneliness, fear, and deep hurt fill the hearts and souls of too many. Sadness, heartbreak, and personal failure can make you feel as if life will never be the same again. Storms will come.

> *Storms can bring shock and destruction. As a bolt of lightning explodes on the earth, trial can explode into your life and create havoc.*

We know why. God didn't hold back the truth. Storms come because we are broken, shattered people, living in a broken and fallen world. The Bible says in Romans 8:22, *"We know that the whole creation has been groaning as in the pains of childbirth right up to the present time."* Paul added, *"And we also groan."* Storms come because this world and our lives are broken by the chaos and frustration of sin.

This is where we need some clarity about the word "sin." Too often "sin" is equated only with misdeeds. We think of sin as saying a few bad words or getting caught up in road rage. Sure, there are big sins like murder and other violent acts, but because only a few people tumble over the really-big-sin edge, we become convinced that sin is primarily about small slip-ups.

That's where we make a major mistake. Sin is much deeper and much darker than a minor faux pas here and there. Sin is a condition. It is a state of twisted reality. Sin means that this world and our lives are out of kilter. Something is very wrong. Everything from the proper function of the earth to the behavior of our genetic system is seriously out of whack. Sin means that our world and lives are by nature chaotic and broken. Why do young people die tragically? Why is there abuse and violence? Why does corruption and unfairness spring up all around the world? Why do disasters wipe out hundreds of thousands of people? Because the world is a mess. We are a mess. Chaos saturates our existence. We are in need of repair. Romans 3:10 tells us that in this condition of sin, *"There is no one righteous, not even one."* We're all fouled up in a very serious way.

How do we survive? We are hanging by the thread of God's kindness. Our lives and this world aren't going down the tubes because God doesn't abandon us. Jesus said in John 16:33, *"In this world you will have trouble. But take heart! I have overcome the world."* Storms will come. There are plenty of them. But Jesus overcame the storms and holds on to us in the midst of the turmoil.

What Makes Suffering, Suffering

But why are struggles so hard? If Jesus is hanging on to us, why is it so difficult to make it through the storms?

A few years ago my family and I were able to take a vacation in the United Kingdom. We decided to sign up for a bus tour from London to Stonehenge. We boarded the vehicle and, as was customary for these tours, there was a guide on the bus. Her name was Carlotta. Her job was to narrate our trip and tell us everything she could think of that would fill us with interesting information about the journey. I was excited about the excursion and thought I knew how long the trip would last—about an hour and a half. One hour passed on the bus. Carlotta was talking the whole time. I thought to myself, "Well, we're almost there." Two hours went by. Carlotta was still talking. Three hours went by. Carlotta was talking about her son and her cat and her sofa, and she was driving me crazy! I didn't know when we would reach our destination. Carlotta never told us. I was hungry. My knees were jammed into the seat in front of me. And Carlotta seemed like she was ready to keep talking all day! I began to think that we were never going to reach our destination, that this trip would never end!

That is exactly what makes suffering, suffering. You begin to believe it's never going to end. What you're going through becomes an impenetrable wall, a hopeless journey. There seems to be no way out. That is the nature of life's storms. That is what true struggle is made of.

Paul described it well in 2 Corinthians 11:28-29. After a list of all his trials he said: *"Besides everything else, I face daily the pressure of my concern for all the churches. Who is weak, and I do not feel weak? Who is led into sin, and I do not inwardly burn?"* Paul was traveling through the storm. He couldn't see an end in sight. He was experiencing the agony of suffering.

Suffering is not waiting too long at a stop light, having your cell phone cut out at an inopportune time, experiencing a bad hair day, or standing around in a slow checkout line at Home Depot. Suffering means that you see no way out. Your struggle seems hopeless and endless.

So, what do you do? Acts chapters 27 and 28 tell the harrowing story of the Apostle Paul's shipwreck while he was on his way to Rome. Verse thirteen of chapter 27 tells us: *"When a gentle south wind began to blow, they thought they had obtained what they wanted; so they weighed anchor and sailed along the shore of Crete."* A gentle south wind came and the sailors sprung into action. This gentle wind would push them to their destination. So they thought. Verse fourteen brings the bad news of the unexpected: *"Before very long, a wind of hurricane force, called the 'northeaster,' swept down from the island."*

The surprise of suffering had begun. For two weeks they were driven by the wind. The ship was out of control. There was no end in sight. What did they do? The same thing you and I do when suffering enters our lives. We try to gain control.

First, the sailors, in the middle of this raging storm, tied ropes around the ship to hold it together. Suffering enters your life and your first reaction is to hold it all together yourself. You may be reacting that way right now. "Hold it together," you tell yourself, "You don't have to share this with anyone." You reach for your bootstraps and determine that you're going to pull yourself out of this. Be tough, be resourceful, shake it off, "stiff upper lip"—as Carlotta would say.

Next, the sailors lowered the sea anchor to slow the ship down. That might be your next reaction to suffering. You might decide to slow down, read a book, take a day off, perhaps go on a vacation. Maybe you feel that you need a break, a little time away from the rigors of life. Those are very good things to do, but they may provide only temporary respite. What if the suffering keeps going?

In Acts 27:18 the sailors started to throw cargo overboard. Some real change was happening on that ship. Perhaps as you face suffering you decide to make some changes, adjust the pace of your life, re-set your priorities. Maybe you throw some old "baggage" overboard. Again, that can be very good. But what if the suffering continues?

In verse nineteen the crew became desperate and heaved essential gear overboard. You might do the same thing. You sacrifice your pride and ego. You give up some parts of your life that you've been holding on to stubbornly. You even agree to talk to a counselor. But the suffering may continue.

Finally, verse twenty may capture how you feel at that point: *"When neither sun nor stars appeared for many days and the storm continued raging, we finally gave up all hope of being saved."* You lose hope. You tried everything, but nothing worked.

Suffering is a strong and relentless adversary. It can defy all your efforts. You do everything possible to deny it, to power up on it, to cope with it, to bargain with it, and to get around it. You may even try to compare your life to other people's experiences in an effort to get a handle on the pace and progression of your own suffering, but then your life takes its own turn. Suffering defies sense, experience, and your strength. It mystifies us. That's why Biblical writers asked, *"How long, O Lord?"* (Psalm 6:3), and *"Why do the nations rage?"* (Acts 4:25) That's why we ask the same questions today. Suffering stumps us. Storms do not make sense. Struggle doesn't provide any easy answers.

What To Do With Suffering

So, what can you do? Wait a minute, we just asked that question. We've just been through what WE do. That's the wrong question to ask. On that tour bus, I couldn't do anything. The people on the ship in Acts 27 were helpless. In your suffering, you are at a loss. That's the problem! It's also what each of us needs to know. We can't solve our suffering. We can't come up with the secrets to overcome the struggles and storms. But there is a fix. There is freedom. There is a solution.

> *Suffering defies sense, experience, and your strength. Suffering stumps us. Storms do not make sense. Struggle doesn't provide any easy answers.*

On our tour, we had a bus driver named Eddie. He was good. Eddie decided that he was going to stop the bus, open the door, and let us get out. I felt like shouting "Hallelujah!" when I walked out that door! Do you know what Eddie did? He put an end to the endlessness. He broke through the wall. He was in the bus with us and provided a way out.

For your life, for your suffering, God the Father sent Jesus to drive the bus. Jesus entered your suffering. He got on the bus. He grew up with all the growing pains parents and children

20

experience. He navigated the way through family conflict and rejection. He went through terrible temptation and attacks by Satan. He felt the heartbreak and tears of grief when a loved one died. He was called names and criticized. He felt the pressure to perform and the scrutiny of people who claimed to be in charge. He was filled with extreme anxiety about His life—to the point of despairing of life itself. Friends betrayed Him. Jesus was physically abused. He experienced physical disability when He was unable to carry His own cross. Jesus even experienced what it is like to die, and worse, what it is to suffer total separation from God—hell itself. And Jesus, on the bus with you, says, "I understand what you're going through. I know every ounce of what you're feeling. I've been there too. I've been through the worst. And I'm with you in this." Jesus shares your burden.

But more than that, Jesus did what no one else could do. He made His way through your suffering to provide a way out. He died, but He rose up from death. Do you see what Jesus accomplished? He made it through the ridicule, the pressure, the temptation, the disability, the grief, the depression, the conflict— even death and hell. He made it through! He ended the endlessness of suffering. And the grace of it all is that He said, "Come with me on my bus! There's an end in sight!" Good-bye Carlotta, hello Jesus! Good-bye endlessness, hello help, hope and life. Would you want to be on the bus with any other driver?

That's what we're going to dig into in this book. We're going to face the struggles head on and see Jesus in action. We're going to see how Jesus is really driving the bus—even in the most extreme and puzzling situations in life. We're going to see how Jesus provides a way out, an open door, new hope and new life.

We're going to discover genuine encouragement in the midst of struggle. We're going to find practical tools for struggling well.

In 2 Corinthians 1:8-9 Paul summed this up well when he said, *"We do not want you to be uninformed, brothers, about the hardships we suffered in the province of Asia. We were under great pressure, far beyond our ability to endure, so that we despaired even of life. Indeed, in our hearts we felt the sentence of death. But this happened that we might not rely on ourselves but on God, who raises the dead."*

In the middle of your struggle, there is hope. The living Jesus enters your life—He gets on the bus. The living and active Word of God brings the Spirit of Christ into your life. The living waters of baptism fill you with the Spirit of God. Jesus enters your life through the gift of Holy Communion. He says, "Come with me. I will bring you safely through." The living Christ is the one who has broken through the paralyzing barriers of storms and struggles. He defeated death! As Paul said, we don't rely on ourselves during suffering. We rely on *"God who raises the dead."*

That's what happened during the shipwreck episode in Acts 27. Trouble broke out as the ship broke up. We hear that *"The soldiers planned to kill the prisoners to prevent any of them from swimming away and escaping. But the centurion wanted to spare Paul's life and kept them from carrying out their plan" (vss. 42-43).* The centurion is a reflection of Christ. He wanted to "spare" Paul's life. The word literally means that he wanted to bring Paul safely through. God promised that everyone would survive the shipwreck, and verse forty-four uses the same verb—everyone was brought safely through. If you are a sufferer, you

22

receive the same promise. Jesus will bring you safely through. He's a good driver. Better than Eddie. He opens up the way for struggling well.

How Will You Struggle?

So, how will you struggle? You can encounter storms and get very grumpy. You can get ornery and bitter. You can throw your hands into the air and act as if there is no God and no hope. You can live as if everything is falling apart. You can become reckless and chase after what the world says will make you happy and whole. Yes, you can struggle poorly, or you can struggle well.

One of my favorite strugglers from the Bible is Jacob. In Genesis chapter 32 we find Jacob scared stiff as he prepared to meet his estranged brother, Esau. Jacob had cheated Esau. Jacob lied to him. Jacob stole Esau's blessing and swindled Esau out of his birthright. Now Jacob was coming back home. He prayed a desperate prayer in verses nine through twelve:

> *So, how will you struggle? You can throw your hands into the air and act as if there is no God and no hope. Yes, you can struggle poorly, or you can struggle well.*

O God of my father Abraham, God of my father Isaac, O LORD, who said to me, "Go back to your country and your relatives, and I will make you prosper," I am unworthy of all the kindness and faithfulness you have shown your servant. I had only my staff when I crossed this Jordan, but now I have become two groups. Save me,

23

I pray, from the hand of my brother Esau, for I am afraid he will come and attack me, and also the mothers with their children. But you have said, "I will surely make you prosper and will make your descendants like the sand of the sea, which cannot be counted."

Jacob was shaken to his core. He went to sleep that night, struggling with what lay before him. Genesis 32 goes on:

So Jacob was left alone, and a man wrestled with him till daybreak. When the man saw that he could not overpower him, he touched the socket of Jacob's hip so that his hip was wrenched as he wrestled with the man. Then the man said, "Let me go, for it is daybreak." But Jacob replied, "I will not let you go unless you bless me." The man asked him, "What is your name?" "Jacob," he answered. Then the man said, "Your name will no longer be Jacob, but Israel, because you have struggled with God and with men and have overcome" (vss. 24-28).

Jacob wrestled with God. He held onto God's promise and didn't let go until he received God's blessing. Jacob traveled steadily—tenaciously—along God's path and wouldn't give up until God's help, encouragement, and presence were revealed. He didn't run. He didn't lie. He didn't change his mind. He didn't veer off God's calling and path to return home. He struggled well.

The beautiful fact is that God renamed Jacob "Israel." We now know all of God's people as "the people of Israel." Paul even includes Gentiles in the company of those called "Israel" (Ephesians 3:6). What is the meaning of the word "Israel"? It means: "He struggles with God." The central identity of God's people, the name God gave his precious redeemed, shows that we are called to struggle well. We are invited to hold onto God during the struggle and to insist on His blessing.

This calls for a deep and courageous perspective toward life. Life is more than simply the here and now. Satisfaction and blessing come from more than ease and prosperity. Making a difference in life springs not only from visible impact, but from the invisible contest happening in this spiritual world. Ones who struggle well trust that God will bring them farther than they could go on their own.

Elijah saw that reality during his struggles. After he defeated and killed the prophets of Baal, Queen Jezebel threatened and intimidated Elijah. She told him, *"May the gods deal with me, be it ever so severely, if by this time tomorrow I do not make your life like that of one of them" (1 Kings 19:2).* Verse three says that Elijah ran for his life:

> *When he came to Beersheba in Judah, he left his servant there, while he himself went a day's journey into the desert. He came to a broom tree, sat down under it and prayed that he might die. "I have had enough, LORD," he said. "Take my life; I am no better than my ancestors" (vss. 3-4).*

Under his own power, Elijah traveled one day, lay down under a tree in despair, and fell asleep. Verse five continues:

> *All at once an angel touched him and said, "Get up and eat." He looked around, and there by his head was a cake of bread baked over hot coals, and a jar of water. He ate*

and drank and then lay down again. The angel of the LORD came back a second time and touched him and said, "Get up and eat, for the journey is too much for you" (vss.5-7).

The journey was too much for Elijah. But it was not too much for God. The Lord showed Elijah a life that was deep, full, and miraculous. It was life given by Him:

So he got up and ate and drank. Strengthened by that food, he traveled forty days and forty nights until he reached Horeb, the mountain of God. There he went into a cave and spent the night. And the word of the LORD came to him: "What are you doing here, Elijah?" (vss. 8-9)

Elijah traveled one day under his own power and was exhausted. God fed him one meal and Elijah was able to travel forty day and forty nights. God's question, "What are you doing here?" can also be translated, "How did you get here?" God was letting Elijah know that there was something more happening during the struggle. There was a deeper and more substantive power at work in his life. God was drawing him close, caring for him, and accomplishing a wonderful plan. Elijah made it to the place where God spoke to him because God brought him there.

God provides you with the same divine fuel. He draws close to you during the storms. He opens doors when you think you're trapped. He gives you all you need to struggle well.

Let's find out how.

Study Guide for Chapter 1:
Struggle Well

1. Is the world a good place or a bad place? Discuss your thoughts about each option.

2. Read Romans 3:9-18. How do these verses clarify the dire reality of sin in our world?

3. What evidence of the chaotic brokenness of life do you see on a day to day basis?

4. How does this sinful and chaotic condition contribute to your struggles?

5. What are your typical reactions when you face a struggle? Describe ways you struggle poorly and struggle well.

6. What helps you respond to struggles better?

7. Read Genesis 18:16-33. In these verses, Abraham "wrestles" with God. Identify statements from Abraham that indicate he struggled well.

8. What does this episode teach you about handling your struggles?

9. Read Hebrews 2:18. This verse talks about Jesus. How does His suffering help you through yours?

10. Share how you have experienced God's "divine fuel" during times of draining adversity.

Chapter Two
Struggle Well
by Recalibrating Expectations

---

*"In this world you will have trouble. But take heart! I have
overcome the world." John 16:33*

*"Dear friends, do not be surprised at the painful trial you are
suffering, as though something strange were happening to you.
But rejoice that you participate in the sufferings of Christ, so that
you may be overjoyed when his glory is revealed." 1 Peter 4:12-13*

Devastating Reality

On February 28, 2009, Nick Schuyler boarded a friend's
boat for a fishing trip in the Gulf of Mexico. Joining Nick and the
owner of the boat were two other friends. The young men were in
their twenties, fit, healthy, and strong. Two were professional
football players. They were ready to have a fun day at sea.

But then disaster struck. As a cold front pushed a storm
closer, the group decided to head back to the Florida coast. But the
boat's anchor was stuck. After attempting to free the anchor for
nearly an hour, the group made one last desperate attempt by tying
the anchor rope to the stern and gunning the engine. Suddenly, the
stern sank into the gray water, swamping and capsizing the boat.
The four men were thrown into the sixty-four-degree Gulf.
Shocked and frightened, they clung to the boat.

In his book, <u>Not Without Hope</u>, Nick Schuyler tells his story of survival at sea after the horrible mishap. His three companions died—two of them in his arms. He was battered by waves and storms. He was wracked with hunger and thirst. He waited and prayed for help for forty-three hours.

During his ordeal he hoped for the best, but everything kept going wrong. He said, "It seemed like every time I thought it couldn't get any worse, it got worse" (<u>Not Without Hope</u>, William Morrow, 2010, p.141). The boat capsized. Supplies were impossible to retrieve. Cell phones didn't work. Flares were unusable. Twelve to fifteen foot waves pounded the struggling men. It was impossible to swim for help. The weather got colder and colder. One man died, then the second, then Nick's best friend.

Nick said that he kept screaming, "Why, God, why? Please, God, let this be a bad dream...Let me wake up already...Why?" (pp.139-140)

What is Normal?

That question has echoed throughout the centuries. It reverberates through inner city streets, hospital hallways, small villages in the far reaches of the world, and in the hearts of sufferers everywhere. Why? Life seems so random. Life is so chaotic. Life is so unfair.

We believe it shouldn't be that way. We believe life should be much better. Perhaps we hold to that belief because, as Ecclesiastes 3:11 says, *"[God] has...set eternity in the hearts of men."* We know there is something good and whole and complete out there. We yearn for that. We look for it.

But life on this side of eternity shows us something different. It shows us that hurt, pain, difficulties, and mishaps are normal. Bad news is not an uncommon exception. It happens all the time.

For some reason, however, we wake up in the morning thinking that everything will go smoothly and that nothing will go wrong. Sure, there will be some bumps along the way, but those will be exceptions, not the rule. Then we encounter reality. Complications abound. The unexpected happens. Schedules are hardly ever accurate. Sickness surprises us. We oversleep. The kids don't cooperate. The project costs twice as much and takes triple the estimated time. Disaster, injustice, and violence run rampant. Life is a mess.

And this reality, this state of being, is completely normal.

As you are well aware, this normal state of affairs, this mess, is not simply lighthearted inconvenience. Normal life brings crushing hurt. It involves deep wounds and turbulent storms.

If any book puts normal life on display it is the Bible. The Bible is a narrative about real life. It is not a collection of the biographies of perfect people living in paradise. That only lasted for the first two pages. The rest of the Bible shows us in a bold and clear way that normal life is not easy. In one account after another, the Bible shows that crazy, confused, and crushing circumstances abound. You can expect struggle.

The good news is that the Divine stepped into this mess. God is with you as a helper, savior and friend. Psalm 46:1 says it well: *"God is our refuge and strength, an ever-present help in trouble."* Help in trouble. It's an accurate summary of normal life. Trouble is real and we need help.

Great Expectations?

What are your expectations in life? I'm not a pessimist. I definitely see the glass as half full. I'm a pretty cheerful guy. Most mornings I wake up and hit the ground running—literally! I like to have a positive outlook and a can-do spirit. But sometimes my expectations are way off base. Sometimes I forget about the storms that come. Sometimes I'm not prepared for the hurt. Many times I am surprised and caught off guard by struggles.

I've been warned about that. Ecclesiastes 5:8 says, *"If you see the poor oppressed in a district, and justice and rights denied, do not be surprised at such things."* Peter warned in 1 Peter 4:12, *"Dear friends, do not be surprised at the painful trial you are suffering, as though something strange were happening to you."* The Apostle John emphasized that the world didn't offer a welcome mat to Christians: *"Do not be surprised, my brothers, if the world hates you"* (1 John 3:13).

But somehow, my expectations get off track. Too often I become mystified when everything doesn't go smoothly. I can become frustrated and foul-mooded when life doesn't go my way. And I know I'm not alone.

Recalibrating Expectations

One way to struggle well is to recalibrate expectations. This doesn't mean you have to become a brooding naysayer, speaking doom into every situation. It doesn't mean you live without hope. It simply means that you remember the reality of what is normal in this world. Perfection is not in the here and now.

Your mood, demeanor and character cannot depend on everything going smoothly this side of heaven. Your realistic viewpoint knows better than that.

But there's more. You also realize that struggle does not necessarily mean defeat. Pain can actually lead to gain. Adversity can serve as a tool for growth and maturity. Suffering may lead to a deep and mysteriously sweet sense of what life is really all about. Beyond the daily concerns and cares, more important than money and possessions, far and away more significant than status and the approval of the world, is an ultimate purpose for your life. Along with the blessing, joy, and delight of this life; in the mix of pain and challenge, each one of us has an important and eternal reason for being far beyond what we can fully comprehend.

Daniel discovered that. You remember Daniel. As an old man he was tossed into a den of lions and came out unscathed. Decades before the lion's den, however, Daniel was a newly captured boy from Jerusalem, held prisoner by King Nebuchadnezzar of Babylon. Life had gone terribly wrong for young Daniel. He had a bright future ahead of him. He was well educated, wealthy, and was being groomed for leadership in the ranks of Judean royalty. He was handsome and would soon have his pick of princesses. Then it all came crashing down. Babylon besieged Jerusalem and took the best of the best for service in that far away land. Nebuchadnezzar would not let talent go to waste. Daniel was part of a select group of captives that would be transformed into Babylonians.

This was not like moving from Illinois to Texas. Daniel was put into the position of forsaking everything he held precious and of compromising every shred of personal value and belief. As

33

a teenage boy, he was being told to give up his personal identity, his family, and his faith in God. Daniel's future was stolen. His hopes were taken into captivity. He was plunged into a lifetime of struggle. Was there a reason to go on? Could he expect anything out of life anymore?

The Apostle Paul experienced a recalibration of his expectations, too. From the starting point of his dramatic conversion, Paul received a reality check. After Jesus stopped Paul in his treacherous tracks, Jesus commanded Ananias to go to Paul to heal and baptize him. When Ananias objected to reaching out to persecutor Paul, Jesus said, *"Go! This man is my chosen instrument to carry my name before the Gentiles and their kings and before the people of Israel. I will show him how much he must suffer for my name" (Acts 9:15).* Thus Paul began his life of suffering and struggle.

The Apostle described his reality in 2 Corinthians 11:

I have worked much harder, been in prison more frequently, been flogged more severely, and been exposed to death again and again. Five times I received from the Jews the forty lashes minus one. Three times I was beaten with rods, once I was stoned, three times I was shipwrecked, I spent a night and a day in the open sea. I have been constantly on the move. I have been in danger from rivers, in danger from bandits, in danger from my own countrymen, in danger from Gentiles; in danger in the city, in danger in the country, in danger at sea; and in danger from false brothers. I have labored and toiled and have often gone without sleep; I have known hunger and thirst and have often gone without food; I have been cold and naked (vss. 23-27).

Normal life was brutal for Paul. Even worse, Paul struggled with a "thorn in the flesh," an awful affliction that caused crippling difficulty in his life. We don't know what the thorn was, but Paul referenced it as his ever-present reality: *"To keep me from becoming conceited because of these surpassingly great revelations, there was given me a thorn in my flesh, a messenger of Satan, to torment me. Three times I pleaded with the Lord to take it away from me. But he said to me, 'My grace is sufficient for you, for my power is made perfect in weakness'" (2 Corinthians 12:7-9).* For Paul, struggle was normal. It was what he could expect in life.

Then there is Jesus. What assessment of realistic expectations would be complete without looking at the life of Jesus? A professor of mine used to say, "Jesus is more man than any of us." In other words, if you want to understand what it really means to be human, look at Jesus. And, if you want to understand the true nature of life in this broken world, Jesus is the one to look at very carefully.

In Isaiah 53 the coming Messiah was called "a man of sorrows" (vs. 3). He was born as an outcast. His entry into ministry meant plunging into intense temptation from the devil. His final prayers were so stressful that capillaries burst in his forehead and blood mingled with his sweat. His death was cruel, hateful, and unjust. His final cry expressed the devastating agony of being forsaken by God. Jesus walked the pathway of normal, messy, broken reality. That's why He came.

Do You Believe in Brokenness?

As I said, I'm not trying to depress you. It's just that if you are going to struggle well, you need to know what to expect. You need to be aware of the real nature of life. You need to be ready when life starts to crumble in little ways and in big ways. Because it will. If you respond by crumbling along with it, struggle will overwhelm you and chart your course for the future. If you are suddenly shocked and surprised when adversity comes your way, suffering will smother you and make you useless.

> *If you are suddenly shocked and surprised when adversity comes your way, suffering will smother you and make you useless.*

But if you know what is really normal, if your expectations are realistic, then you'll have a chance.

You may say to yourself, "Why, of course I know that life is a challenge. I've been through hard times. I've experienced tragedy in my life. I read about it and hear about it every day. Of course I believe in brokenness."

But each of us forgets so easily. Even as I write this book, I forget that life is an ongoing struggle. You might imagine that, as an author, I get to write in the peace and solitude of a tropical island somewhere. I awake in the morning to the sounds of tropical birds, gentle waves, and warm breezes that rustle the swaying palm trees. After a lavish breakfast of fresh fruit and imported San Antonio breakfast tacos, I stroll along the beach and watch the sunrise for inspiration. Wrong!

I'm writing on the run. My schedule is packed. The phone is ringing. E-mails are streaming into my inbox. There are bills to pay and meetings to attend. I was summoned for jury duty on a day when I was supposed to be writing, so I'm squeezing in a few paragraphs as I wait to be called to a courtroom. Life is crazy! But even as I started to write this paragraph I was expecting a long stretch of quiet concentration and productive writing. I was hoping to finish one chapter during each day I designated for working on this book. But, of course, my plans didn't work out. What happened when I started to fall behind? I got frustrated. I started to get a little grouchy. I was sulking. Why? Because even though I believe in brokenness, even though I am fully aware of this world's fallen state, even though I understand that life isn't smooth, my expectations always seem to get reset to a "perfection mode." Somehow I expect my life to function as it would have before the fall into sin. For some reason, my expectations become inaccurate and I then react with shock, disappointment, grouchiness, and frustration when everything doesn't go my way. I don't think of the deeper purpose. I don't pause to evaluate what opportunities for growth my challenges might present.

In other words, I do not struggle well.

Recalibrating Expectations

This calls for a reality check when struggles strike. It calls for ongoing recalibration of expectations during times of suffering. I mentioned earlier that I am a runner. Since 1991 I've tracked my weekly running mileage. In addition to using a running journal, I graph my total miles for each week throughout the year. Call me a fanatic, but I get motivated by tracking how I'm doing. I have a unique running mileage graph for each year since 1991. Every

37

graph is different, but there is one characteristic all of them have in common: they are filled with ups and downs. Each graph looks like a series of mountain peaks and valleys. Some weeks have high mileage. I was feeling good and going far. Other weeks have low mileage. I was fighting the flu or was injured. Many weeks are in-between. But there are not many consistently straight lines. In my experience, running is all about ups and downs.

What if you graphed your life? What if you charted all the high points, low points and in-between points? How might your life-graph look? There would be mountain peaks. These might include some precious friendships, a few awards or victories in school, a graduation here and there. You might mark times of blessing like getting married and having children. There would also be valleys. You might write down times of illness, the loss of a job, or grief when a precious loved one died. You might remember a classmate or boss who tormented you. You might recall a time of depression or a season of financial struggle. Perhaps a broken relationship would show up as a low point.

Your life chart would look like one of my running charts. It would be filled with ups and downs. There would be seasons of joy and seasons of sorrow. There would be good times and bad times. King Solomon captured this truth about life in Ecclesiastes chapter 3: *"There is a time for everything, and a season for every activity under heaven: A time to be born and a time to die, a time to plant and a time to uproot, a time to kill and a time to heal, a time to tear down and a time to build, a time to weep and a time to laugh, a time to mourn and a time to dance" (vss. 1-4).*

I remember talking with a man who was in his eighties. He was looking back on his life and made a casual comment that stopped me in my tracks. He was describing a difficult time in his marriage due to his wife's health struggles. He said, "That episode was over after about twenty years; then we could really get going and enjoy life again." Twenty years! At the time, I thought a semester with a crummy psychology teacher was bad!

This man recognized what Solomon did: life is a succession of seasons. We need to expect ups and downs.

The danger we face is that we may forget the real rhythm of life. It is very easy to be captured by each moment, by each season. When all is well, you can begin to believe that you're indestructible, that life will never change. During the "up" times you can forget how fragile life is, how thankful you need to be, and how humble you need to stay. And when you traverse the low points, when everything seems to have come

> *The big question you face is: Are you willing to accept temporary uncertainty and pain for a bigger purpose, God's mission for you on this earth?*

crashing down, you can become captured by hopelessness. You may begin to define your life by your strained relationship, extended illness, terrible job, personal failure, or aching soul. You can become bitter and believe that the bad times will never end.

But seasons do not define your life. At the end of a running season, the total outcome is not determined by a mileage peak or valley. There is a bigger picture. The journey was filled with ups and downs, but ups and downs do not tell the whole story. The big question you face is: Are you willing to accept temporary uncertainty and pain for a bigger purpose, God's mission for you on this earth? Are you willing to live through the peaks and valleys, the ups and downs, without losing hope? Are you willing to trust that God has a plan—even in your seasons of suffering?

How Can You Struggle Well?

On your own, it would be very easy to lose hope, to give up, to collapse in despair, or to lash out in rage. With your own limited view, it would be natural to believe that there's nothing deeper than what you can see. The difference is made when Jesus enters the picture. Jesus was a truth teller. When He said, *"I am the way and the truth and the life" (John 14:6),* part of being the truth meant leveling with us about the disappointment and brokenness of the here and now. Jesus' message is not easy to hear. It brings us to our knees and exposes our every imperfection and weakness. But there's another part of the truth.

Remember Daniel's struggle. After he was confronted with the crushing news that his diet was going to be changed from the ceremonially clean menu of his home to the unclean and God-dishonoring Babylonian fare, Daniel chapter 1 tells us:

> *But Daniel resolved not to defile himself with the royal food and wine, and he asked the chief official for permission not to defile himself this way. Now God had caused the official to show favor and sympathy to Daniel, but the official told Daniel, "I am afraid of my lord the king, who has assigned your food and drink. Why should he see you looking worse than the other young men your age? The king would then have my head because of you." Daniel then said to the guard whom the chief official had appointed over Daniel, Hananiah, Mishael and Azariah,*

"Please test your servants for ten days: Give us nothing but vegetables to eat and water to drink. Then compare our appearance with that of the young men who eat the royal food, and treat your servants in accordance with what you see." So he agreed to this and tested them for ten days. At the end of the ten days they looked healthier and better nourished than any of the young men who ate the royal food" (vss. 8-15).

In the middle of the worst adversity, God stepped in to do something remarkable. Time after time, when struggle hit hard, God opened up a new way. It was not only a way of survival, but a way of mission. God wanted more than an easy life of comfort and entertainment for young Daniel and his friends. There was a world in need. People were lost. Babylonians needed the living God who saves. It was only through struggle that Daniel and his countrymen were able to display God's help and rescue to a nation that needed it.

You may remember the defiant words of Daniel's friends Shadrach, Meshach and Abednego. After being threatened with death in a fiery furnace because they refused to worship the king's image of gold, the three young men declared, *"O Nebuchadnezzar, we do not need to defend ourselves before you in this matter. If we are thrown into the blazing furnace, the God we serve is able to save us from it, and he will rescue us from your hand, O king. But even if he does not, we want you to know, O king, that we will not serve your gods or worship the image of gold you have set up" (Daniel 3:16-18).*

Struggle intensified. They were tossed into the inferno. But God came through. The angel of the Lord stood with the men

41

and protected them from the fire. They emerged from the furnace without a hair singed or the smell of smoke on them. King Nebuchadnezzar was flabbergasted. But the young men's season of suffering resulted in the king's proclamation throughout the land that their God was the God who saves. Struggle became the normal way of life for Daniel and the captives of Babylon, but so did the opportunities to make an eternal difference in the lives of others through God's help and rescue.

The same was true for Paul. Yes, he suffered extreme hardship and he wrestled with his thorn in the flesh. But Jesus stepped in to strengthen him. After lamenting his suffering, Paul declared: *"But [the Lord] said to me, 'My grace is sufficient for you, for my power is made perfect in weakness.' Therefore I will boast all the more gladly about my weaknesses, so that Christ's power may rest on me. That is why, for Christ's sake, I delight in weaknesses, in insults, in hardships, in persecutions, in difficulties. For when I am weak, then I am strong" (2 Corinthians 12:9-10).* Struggle was normal, but Jesus made His help, strength, and the accomplishment of His mission normal, too. There was another side to the brutal truth of suffering. God was at work.

God's work through suffering was most evident in the life of Jesus. The Man of Sorrows stepped into the horribly normal chaos of our sin-stained world. He carried the burden of all rebellion, pain, and struggle. But Jesus rose from the dead! He broke through the struggle so that, as Romans 6:4 says, *"We too, may live a new life."* Struggle did not have the last word. The valley of death did not define our lives. Paul emphasized this new normal in 1 Corinthians 15:20-22, *"But Christ has indeed been raised from the dead, the firstfruits of those who have fallen asleep.*

For since death came through a man, the resurrection of the dead comes also through a man. For as in Adam all die, so in Christ all will be made alive."

There is a bigger picture to suffering. More is happening than meets the eye. Struggles are connected to the eternal work of God. He never wanted suffering and pain to invade our lives, but He will work through it to accomplish His will. That's one reason you can struggle well. As you expect chaos and brokenness, you can also expect God's work in the middle of it. Your time on this earth includes not only loss, but life; not only pain, but promise; not only suffering, but strength.

Getting Through

So how can you survive this see-saw battle of reality? If you can hardly get out of bed in the morning because of your emotional fatigue, if you are being overtaken by inner turmoil, how do you get through the barriers of suffering when they seem so insurmountable?

There is a way. I saw it clearly on vacation a few years ago. As I embarked on a familiar running course one morning, I was filled with mixed emotions. We had been coming to this vacation spot for many years. The running course I chose that morning was one of my favorites. It went around a small and picturesque lake. What better view could there be than the mist on the lake in the morning? What wonders of creation could be more stirring than the sounds of loons and the sight of a great blue heron searching for its breakfast? But as I began my sunrise sojourn, I couldn't help but dread one part of this run. It was the north end of the lake. As I turned right at a state park, I had to navigate my way down a busy county road. The road ran next to the lake. For about

43

a quarter of a mile, there was no room for pedestrians. With no shoulder, I had to either balance on a thin strip of sand that sloped steeply into the water, or I had to take a chance, stay on the road, and watch for cars. The pathway became even worse after that treacherous section. In order to make it around the final curve of this portion of the running course, I had to climb a small hill where all the sand and gravel from the road washed onto the shoulder. There was always plenty of mud and very difficult terrain at this point. In order to get past it, I would have to hop up onto the road and take my chances that fast-moving vehicles wouldn't be barreling toward me from the blind curves ahead and behind. This was an awful, nearly impassable barrier.

But my recent visit surprised me. As I turned right at the state park, I saw before me a wide white sidewalk! A sidewalk! I thought it must be just a short addition next to the state park so campers could cross the street. Surely it couldn't last. But I was wrong. The sidewalk continued! It went all the way around the north end of the lake, past the dangerous hill, and up to the road that led to the safe and peaceful part of the course. The sidewalk was beautiful and new! It even had a railing next to it for extra safety.

Then I saw how this new way became possible. As I ran past the blind curve, I saw a cross. It had printed on it, "Logan, June 2004." During that summer, a little boy named Logan was riding his bike around the north end of the lake. At the most treacherous section, a car hit him and killed him. His parents and the whole community got together to raise funds for the construction of a safe sidewalk around the north end of the lake. They called it "Logan's Walk."

For years people struggled with this dangerous part of the course around the lake. The city didn't have the resources to address the issue. Individuals wouldn't have thought of trying to fix this problem. But then a young boy died. And his death made a way through.

That's what Jesus did for you. He died to make a way through the barriers of suffering and struggle. He broke through the darkness to give you the new pathway of light and life. He created new possibilities even in the midst of suffering. He showed that the worst of suffering can give birth to the greatest blessing. With His death and resurrection, Jesus changed our perspective. He provided a new pathway for life's journey. Because of Him, we can struggle well.

That's what Paul was talking about in 1 Corinthians 15. The resurrection of Jesus, Paul emphasized, means that we don't have to give up. In the face of hardship—and even death, Jesus will bring us through. Chapter 15 concludes: *"Where, O death, is your victory? Where, O death is your sting? The sting of death is sin, and power of sin is the law. But thanks be to God! He gives us the victory through our Lord Jesus Christ. Therefore, my dear brothers, stand firm. Let nothing move you. Always give yourselves fully to the work of the Lord, because you know that your labor in the Lord is not in vain"* (1 Corinthians 15:55-58).

Jesus is alive, therefore your labor in the Lord is not in vain. Your struggle is not a waste of time. Your expectations have been transformed. Even as pain fills your heart and soul, the certainty of greater hope and purpose can provide balance and clarity. You don't have to give up. You don't have to collapse. You don't have to spin out of control. You can struggle well. You can struggle well because you know that God does not fail you–even though it looks like He has.

Author and Pastor Helmut Thielicke wrote about the new perspective God gives. He said, "Rebellion and persecution are not at all a sign that Christ has departed and left the battlefield of the world to the opposing forces. On the contrary, all this is a sign that he is coming, indeed, that he is very near" (<u>Man in God's World,</u> 1963, p.195). In the middle of disaster, God lets you know that disaster is His specialty. He is close to you. He is your hope.

> *You can struggle well because you know that God does not fail you–even though it looks like He has.*

Thielicke went on, "Despite terror, persecution, and catastrophe, the cry [of the Bible] is not, 'Watch out! Take cover!' but rather the vibrant message, 'Lift up your heads, for your redemption draws near.' The darker it gets, the nearer the day, and the closer God is to you with his surprises. What the godless see as a confirmation of the 'death of God'...becomes for you a confirmation that the Lord is near, that He is coming to meet you from the other side" (<u>How Modern Should Theology Be?,</u> 1969, pp.73-74).

Because of Jesus, you can look struggle straight in the eye—even with fear and pain and trembling, and still lift up your head to see Jesus nearby. Because of Jesus, you can be confident that there is a plan and mission for your life, a significant purpose for your existence, even when—especially when—you are doubled over in disillusionment and disappointment.

Sent to Serve

This is an important balance for an effective life. It may be part of what Paul was talking about when he said, *"I have learned the secret of being content in any and every situation, whether well fed or hungry, whether living in plenty or in want. I can do everything through him who gives me strength"* *(Philippians 4:12-13).*

Circumstances did not dictate Paul's sense of purpose. He had his ups and downs like any of us, but Jesus opened a door in his life to new strength and a new outlook.

Hymn writer John C. Crum captured this balance in his Easter hymn, "Now the Green Blade Rises." In verse four he describes the new creation-reality of life in Jesus even as the corrupt and broken creation is where we reside:

> When our hearts are wintry, grieving, or in pain,
> Your touch can call us back to life again,
> Fields of our hearts that dead and bare have been;
> Love is come again like wheat arising green.

To struggle well means understanding that the broken world will always bring wintry blasts of grief, frustration, and pain, but in that winter chill, Jesus is bringing the hope of springtime.

That reality may be best expressed by what happened in the very beginning. After Adam and Eve disobeyed God and plunged headlong into the new normal of disobedience and decay, God struggled well. He was hurt by the Fall. His heart was grieved when His love was not reciprocated. But instead of lashing out, God began to construct a new creation. Into chaos and failure, He brought promise and purpose.

God declared in Genesis 3:15, *"And I will put enmity between you and the woman, and between your offspring and hers; he will crush your head, and you will strike his heel."* This verse is called the protevangelion—the first Good News. It speaks of God's cosmic plan "B." Creation crumbled, so God would orchestrate a new creation. The "offspring" of the woman mentioned in Genesis 3:15 refers to the coming Savior. Jesus would crush Satan's head, but in the process the Savior would be wounded. God didn't let darkness get Him down. Instead, He made it a venue to shine His light.

Death was a consequence of eating from the tree of the knowledge of good and evil. Fortunately, God accepted substitutes for the lives of the first human beings. Genesis 3:21 tells us, *"The LORD God made garments of skin for Adam and his wife and clothed them."* The blood of animals atoned for the sin of Adam and Eve. God was doing something new. With laser-like focus, God was working to save His precious people.

Next, God dug deep to do something completely surprising. Genesis 3:22-23 says: *"And the LORD God said, 'The man has now become like one of us, knowing good and evil. He must not be allowed to reach out his hand and take also from the tree of life and eat, and live forever.' So the LORD God banished him from the Garden of Eden to work the ground from which he had been taken."*

At first glance, this development seems so sad. Banished? Cut off to fend for themselves? A life of misery in a broken world? Or was something else happening?

The literal translation of verse twenty-three is: *"And Yahweh God SENT him from the Garden of Eden to SERVE the earth from which he was taken."* The word for "sent" is the word we know in the New Testament as "apostello"—apostle! In this verse, Adam and Eve weren't being chastised. They were being sent—just as Jesus sent His followers. This was a commissioning not condemnation. Adam and Eve were the first apostles! They were sent to serve.

The phrase for "work the ground" literally says to "serve the earth." The word for "serve" is used in the book of Isaiah for Jesus the suffering servant, the one who came not to be served, but to serve and to give His life as a ransom for many. Adam and Eve weren't being sentenced to a prison camp. They were being given a purpose—to reach the lost, to bring God's springtime into a sin-wintry world. Adam and Eve were agents of a new creation.

Instead of brooding, condemning, or destroying, God created a chain reaction of life in a dying world. When struggle hit, God struggled well. He didn't get sidetracked from His unfathomable love. He didn't lose His sense of purpose for creation. Everything went haywire, but God stayed focused. Struggle would not win the day. God's grand and glorious plan would prevail. And His plan involved us!

Jesus said to the seventy-two in Luke chapter 10: *"The harvest is plentiful, but the workers are few. Ask the Lord of the harvest, therefore, to send out workers into his harvest field. Go! I am sending you" (Luke 10:2-3a).*

This is life-changing. Yes, you can expect trouble in life. But you don't have to stop there. There's something more, something beautiful. God creates a new set of expectations. Into darkness, he sends light. Into suffering, He sends help. Into brokenness, he sends blessing. Into struggle, He sends Himself—and He sends you!

Instead of losing all hope when hurt hits, you can look deeper. Deep inside the very real and painful challenges of life is an opportunity to experience God's closeness. Woven into the times that test you is God's sending voice, calling you to serve the people in your life as His witness and representative. You may not know what God will do or how He will use you in His plan, but your recalibrated expectations make His action worth looking for. You are not abandoned. You've been sent to struggle well.

Study Guide for Chapter 2:
Struggle Well by Recalibrating Expectations

1. How do your expectations about what life should be like clash with life's reality?

2. How do these clashes affect your mood, your relationships, and your faith?

3. Read Paul's list of struggles in 2 Corinthians 11:23-29. What would you include in your list of struggles?

4. What expectations in your life need to be recalibrated? Talk about how this recalibration will help you.

5. Read Isaiah 53:1-6. Describe how Jesus experienced the stark reality of suffering in the world and what comfort His suffering gives you.

51

6.   What struggles surprise you most?

7.   Read 2 Corinthians 1:3-7. Paul describes a chain reaction of comfort in suffering. How have you been blessed, encouraged, or inspired by the struggles of others?

8.   How have you seen God reach others through your struggles?

9.   Describe how a time of struggle has grown you.

10. How and to whom is God sending you to help and bring His blessings—even as you struggle?

Chapter Three
Struggle Well
by Traveling Steadily

"The salvation of the righteous comes from the LORD; he is their stronghold in time of trouble." Psalm 37:39

"Trouble and distress have come upon me, but your commands are my delight." Psalm 119:143

Weaknesses and Broken Dreams

I want to take you back to 1986. It was my final year at the seminary. My wife and I had been married for three and a half years. In the apartment where we lived our bathroom faucet was leaking. I came home from classes early one day while my wife was still at work. I heard the drip, drip, drip, that would sometimes keep us awake at night and thought to myself, "Wouldn't it be nice to surprise my dear wife by fixing that leaky faucet?" I had read a little about this kind of repair and knew it wouldn't be very complicated, so I got my tools and began this thoughtful project.

I thought I turned the water off. The geyser that shot from the faucet, hit the ceiling, and began to flood the bathroom told me otherwise.

I learned something that fateful day. I am not a plumber. I also saw a key life principle in action. It's a principle that I've seen repeated over and over again in my life: As time goes on, your weaknesses will surface. Have you noticed that principle in your life? The areas in which you need to grow become clear. Your vulnerabilities show up.

This is something everyone experiences. And it's not easy. Joseph of the Old Testament had his weaknesses exposed early on. He was an immature braggart. At seventeen years of age, he was his daddy's favorite. Jacob loved Joseph so much, he was given the famous coat of many colors—*"a richly ornamented robe" (Genesis 37:3).* Joseph started to have some vivid dreams, but instead of pondering their meaning to himself, he recounted them to his older brothers and gloated about how they would one day bow down to him. Genesis 37:8 tells us that because of these dreams, *"they hated him all the more."*

This hatred didn't bode well for young Joseph. It didn't take long for his brothers to begin their plot to kill him. You may know what happened next. Joseph's brother Rueben had second thoughts and convinced the angry mob of men to throw him into an empty well in the desert. When some merchants from the land of Midian came along, another brother, Judah, came up with the idea of selling Joseph as a slave. The merchants paid the brothers twenty pieces of silver and took Joseph to Egypt. The seventeen-year-old boy who was full of himself and on top of the world ended up in a foreign land as a lowly servant for one of Pharaoh's officials, Potiphar, the captain of the guard. Joseph now lived the life of a hated outcast whose dreams were dashed.

A Specific Sinner

Over time, your sins and weaknesses will become very clear. You will see their impact. You will feel their pain. And you won't like it.

We are much more comfortable being sinners "in general" than being specific sinners. Being a sinner "in general" means that you exceed the speed limit with all the cars around you. You're just going with the flow. Being a specific sinner means that you're the one who sees the flashing lights of the police car in your rear view mirror. You're the one who gets the ticket. That doesn't feel good. It's humbling and embarrassing to have your weaknesses and wrongdoing exposed.

When I was growing up, I lived in a neighborhood where a group of boys enjoyed being sinners in general. They loved having the reputation of being the ones who caused trouble. One of their favorite activities was to mess around with our mailboxes. Back then we had mailboxes built into the house. The mailman opened the door on the outside of the house and put the letters in the slot. Inside the house you would open a little door and get your mail. The neighborhood troublemakers liked to put annoying things in people's mailboxes—like old pieces of pizza. One day a boy who lived across the street, Douglas, decided he was going to squeeze some toothpaste into our mailbox. Somehow my mom caught him red handed. Douglas loved being a sinner in general, but when my mom marched him across the street to tell his mom what he had done, he very clearly did not like being a specific sinner.

It doesn't feel good to have your weaknesses, your vulnerabilities, your growth areas, your sins, and your brokenness exposed. In fact, it can be tormenting. But God isn't content to tell you that you're merely a sinner in general. He speaks through His Word to let you know that you are a specific sinner. You have weaknesses, vulnerabilities, habits, and sins that are harmful and that do not give glory to God. Why does God level with you like this? Because He loves you enough to tell you the truth.

God makes life like a stress test. You've heard of a treadmill stress test, haven't you? A cardiologist puts you on a treadmill. Every three minutes he increases the incline and the speed. He doesn't do this to torture you. He does this to expose areas of vulnerability and weakness. As you walk on the treadmill the doctor watches your heart rate, your EKG, and your appearance. He wants to find a hidden weakness that might end up killing you.

> *God makes life like a stress test. He wants to show you areas of life that might be killing you.*

God makes life like a stress test. He wants to show you areas of life that might be killing you—harming your soul. He doesn't do this to torture you; He does this to transform you. He does this to form in you a life that glorifies Him and shines His light. God cares enough to expose your weaknesses. He wants to save you and make you into a person whose life brings His new life to others.

Unfortunately, we do not always struggle well when our weaknesses are exposed. The truth can hurt. That was the result when Jesus taught in the temple. Luke 19:47 says, *"Every day he was teaching at the temple. But the chief priests, the teachers of the law and the leaders among the people were trying to kill him."* Jesus taught very specifically about the needs of the people, but the leaders among them didn't want to hear it. Instead of facing their sin and weakness, they veered off into denial. Instead of desiring change, they wanted to kill the messenger—the one who exposed their weakness.

When your weaknesses are exposed, you may respond with denial. You may have a reaction of self-loathing. You may get angry. You may simply decide that there is no hope for improvement so you might as well stop trying to change. But can there be another way for a weak and weary sinner? Is it possible to struggle well?

A Disappointed Dreamer

In addition to being confronted with his own weaknesses and imperfections, Joseph experienced broken dreams. He thought his life was going to go very well. He was the favored son with some very nice clothes and some strong indications that his future would be more than favorable. Joseph was looking forward to the day when he would be in charge. But in the blink of an eye his dreams were dashed.

We have so many broken dreams in life. I remember when the life of our second daughter was at risk in the early stages of my wife's pregnancy with her. Late one Saturday night I sat in the emergency room wondering if we would lose the baby. I had tears in my eyes as I grieved the loss of my hopes and dreams for our child.

Dashed dreams hurt deeply. You suffer because of a miscarriage. You mourn the death of someone you love. You agonize over a child who rejects you and goes astray. You suffer as random illness wreaks havoc in a loved one's life. You are crushed if you have been victimized by abuse and violence. The pain of these hurts includes dashed dreams.

The pain and loss of being disappointed by someone, of not becoming what you hoped you would, of being passed by for an honor or promotion, of seeing life become less than you had hoped for: these disappointments cause questions and disillusionment. How do you adjust to dashed dreams?

I was speaking with a mother whose son is suffering with a debilitating mental illness. Once a vibrant boy with a clear mind and loving heart, he is now a young man with a clouded brain and a heart filled with rage. His mother's heart is broken. She is struggling with a hurt-filled broken dream.

The cries of a devastated mother can be found in 2 Kings chapter 4. The prophet Elisha was befriended by a woman from the region of Shunem. Wanting to show his favor for the family's hospitality, Elisha asked what blessing could be given to her. Elisha's servant suggested that since the woman and her husband had no son, having a child could be a great blessing. When Elisha announced this gift to the woman, she responded, *"No, my lord. Don't mislead your servant."* This woman had been down the road of hope for a child. Disappointment struck every time. She didn't want to go there again. But in about a year, she gave birth to a son.

Years went by. The family grew closer and the boy grew to be strong and loved. One day, he went out with his father into the fields. Suddenly the boy was struck with a sharp pain inside his head. Servants carried him to his mother. But the mother could do nothing to help him. At noon, the boy died.

After laying the boy on the bed where Elisha usually slept, the woman mounted a donkey and rode to see the man of God. When she reached Elisha, she fell at his feet and said, *"Did I ask you for a son, my lord? Didn't I tell you, 'Don't raise my hopes'?"*

The Shunammite woman's dreams were dashed. She suffered crushing grief and disappointment. She wondered whether it would have been better never to have a son. It seemed so useless, so senseless.

Broken dreams hurt so badly. You see what is possible. You taste what you yearn for. Your heart's desire is within your grasp. Then, in an instant, it is gone.

How do you cope with dashed dreams? How do you handle deep heartbreak and disappointment? Should you harden yourself to hope? Should you become bitter and cynical? Should you discourage any dreaming and sink into the mire of a life that has no room for the delightful, the surprising, or the miraculous? When your dreams are dashed can you struggle well?

Struggle Well by Traveling Steadily

Joseph settled into life as a servant in Egypt. How did he handle the struggle? It appears that he traveled steadily. Genesis 39:1-2 says,

> *Now Joseph had been taken down to Egypt. Potiphar, an Egyptian who was one of Pharaoh's officials, the captain of the guard, bought him from the Ishmaelites who had taken him there. The LORD was with Joseph and he prospered, and he lived in the house of his Egyptian master.*

59

Joseph didn't do anything. There was no bragging, no pride, and no trash-talking. He served and God was with him. God took the lead. Giving up self-reliance and self-centeredness, Joseph took one step at a time and watched for God's faithfulness.

When your dreams are dashed, the first step in handling your disappointment is to do nothing. There is no need to jump to conclusions. There is no need to give up or to consider life a failure. Joseph saw that he couldn't rely on himself. God would have to show His hand.

When your weaknesses are exposed, your first step is to accept the truth. In your weakness, you can watch for God's action. The Lord was with Joseph and he prospered. Joseph didn't cause this prosperity. He had no control over anything at this point in his life. God was taking Joseph down a new path.

In chapter one I told you about my encounter with Psalm 37:34 *"Don't be impatient for the Lord to act! Travel steadily along his path."* What was God doing with Joseph? He was leading him to travel steadily. Genesis 39 gives us more detail:

> *When his master saw that the LORD was with him and that the LORD gave him success in everything he did, Joseph found favor in his eyes and became his attendant. Potiphar put him in charge of his household, and he entrusted to his care everything he owned. From the time he put him in charge of his household and of all that he owned, the LORD blessed the household of the Egyptian because of Joseph. The blessing of the LORD was on everything Potiphar had, both in the house and in the field.*

Perhaps for the first time in his life, Joseph saw he had a specific Savior. God knew him. God saw him. God cared about him. God was with him. Joseph simply received the gift of God's care and favor. Joseph got up each morning and watched God in action. He struggled well by traveling steadily with a specific Savior, God who called him by name and walked with him.

You have a specific Savior, too. As you are sobered by your shortcomings and made weary by your weaknesses, Jesus is with you. When you hurt because of heartbreak and are downhearted with disappointment, Jesus knows your suffering and carries you in His arms.

> *You have a specific Savior. As you are sobered by your shortcomings and made weary by your weaknesses, Jesus is with you.*

Think about Jesus' ministry. He saw people's specific needs. He met a person who was blind and He gave him sight. He encountered a person cast aside because of leprosy and cleansed him. He cast demons out of the demon possessed. He restored the woman caught in adultery. He transformed the life of Zacchaeus from selfish swindler to grateful giver. Jesus is a specific Savior.

Remember when Jesus hung on the cross between two thieves. One thief was trapped in denial. The other saw his weakness. He cried out to Jesus, *"Jesus, remember me when you come into your kingdom."* Jesus didn't respond by saying, "I am dying for the sins of the world in general." It's true that Jesus died for the sins of the whole world. But on the cross Jesus looked this criminal in the eyes and said, *"I tell you the truth, today you will be*

61

with me in paradise" (Luke 23:43). "You will be with me! My salvation is for YOU!" Jesus is a specific Savior.

As you wait for God to act in the middle of your failure and pain, you can travel steadily along His path. It is a path of dependable forgiveness and eternal hope. When you can't function any more, Jesus is at work. When you feel like you want to lash out, let loose, or throw in the towel, you can stop and know that Jesus is in action for you.

Psalm 4:4 says, *"In your anger do not sin; when you are on your beds, search your hearts and be silent."* In other words, travel steadily. When you feel like losing it, be still. Struggle is not a time to jump to conclusions; it is a time to be quiet and watch for God.

Joseph traveled steadily by watching God in action. He also traveled steadily by following in God's steps. Once success and blessing came Joseph's way, life continued to get complicated. Genesis 39 goes on:

> *Now Joseph was well-built and handsome, and after a while his master's wife took notice of Joseph and said, "Come to bed with me!" But he refused. "With me in charge," he told her, "my master does not concern himself with anything in the house; everything he owns he has entrusted to my care. No one is greater in this house than I am. My master has withheld nothing from me except you, because you are his wife. How then could I do such a wicked thing and sin against God?" And though she spoke to Joseph day after day, he refused to go to bed with her or even be with her. (vss.6-10)*

Joseph was in a faraway land, living with people who didn't know his background. He was cut off from his future and, as a slave, knew he would not get it back. He could have thrown caution to the wind and indulged in what was being offered to him. Instead, he traveled steadily along God's path. He lived with integrity. How could he sin against God when God was so faithful to him?

Life brings deep feelings. They scream out to be satisfied. Like Joseph, you are faced with challenges. With no sure answers, will you stay the course with God on the journey He's given you? As you experience seasons of struggle and emptiness, will you delay immediate gratification to travel steadily along God's path?

The grieving Shunammite woman refused to let her struggle dictate where she traveled. After going to Elisha, the woman insisted on clinging to hope through this man of God. She said to Elisha, *"As surely as the LORD lives and as you live, I will not leave you" (2 Kings 4:30).* It's a strange Biblical account. After Elisha prayed and stretched out on top of the boy's corpse two times, the boy's body warmed. He sneezed seven times and came back to life.

Why did such a random and odd chain of events happen? Infertility, the gift of a son, a tragic death, and a strange resurrection? Because that is what life is like. It's strange and unpredictable. It tries and tests you. Through it all, God steps in with miracles.

As you experience the chaotic and wait upon the miraculous, will you travel steadily? Will you struggle well?

Psalm 37:4 gave me perspective. It lifted me above my feelings and directed me on a journey led by my Savior. After I first heard the verse, I typed it into my electronic calendar so I could read it every day. I needed this regular reminder as the ups and downs of life took me on a roller coaster ride. *"Don't be impatient for the Lord to act! Travel steadily along his path."*

When I became frustrated and felt like lashing out, I heard God's call to travel steadily along His path. When I felt like giving up hope, I saw that life was not at a standstill. God was on the move. My Savior was forging ahead. Struggling well meant going slowly and steadily down a pathway that had no mileage markers and that allowed me to see only the step I was taking. It meant focusing on God's ways and following him. It meant being determined to serve God in the moment and finish well after all was said and done. But it wasn't easy and it wasn't fast.

Microwave and Crockpot Lives

I heard author and pastor John Maxwell speak about two kinds of faith-lives: microwave and crock-pot. A microwave faith-life is what we may expect in our drive-thru, fast food, instant-everything world. Like zapping a quick meal, this kind of walk with God expects quick action and speedy solutions. Patience? I need it now. Closeness to God? Hurry up and give it to me. Resolution to a problem? I don't want to wait. The microwave life is a relationship with God on the run. You've got plenty to do, so God better keep up. You've got no time for prolonged inconvenience. You want to serve God in big ways and accomplish big things. There's no room for messing around.

Unfortunately, the microwave life doesn't grow you or sustain you through struggle. Because it is rooted in your schedule, your agenda, and your convenience, it never goes where God is leading you. It's simply a dose of religion here and there on the course you're choosing.

A crock-pot faith-life is different. You know how a crock-pot works. It's all about waiting. It's all about time. Put some meat, veggies, and water in the crock-pot in the morning, turn it on, and something magical happens. As the hours tick away, slow cooking takes over. A delicious aroma begins to fill the house. The juices flow. The flavors become rich. The food slowly becomes a succulent, melt-in-your-mouth meal.

A crock-pot faith-life takes time. You learn, endure, and grow. When the heat of adversity hits, God works on you. He refines you. He disciples you. Sometimes you succeed and sometimes you fail, but through it all, the Holy Spirit teaches you and matures you. The blessings and challenges saturate your heart and soul. Your spirit becomes rich with God-flavors. Even in the most difficult times—yes, even in your failures—God uses you to bring His presence and influence everywhere you go.

> *Traveling steadily along God's path means living a crock-pot life. You give Him time to run the show.*

Traveling steadily along God's path means living a crock-pot life. You give Him time to run the show. You watch for the ways He is growing you. You talk to Him about His desires for your life. You listen to His Word for direction and strength. You stop and wait upon Him.

King David captured the ups and downs, the ebb and flow, of a walk with God in Psalm 27. At the end of the Psalm, after talking about the joys of being in God's presence and the trials of meeting adversity, David declared, *"Wait for the LORD; be strong and take heart and wait for the LORD" (vs. 14).* Traveling steadily along God's path means looking to God and His ways and waiting for His leadership when life is crumbling or when temptation is calling. As you are led by your faithful Savior, you'll see that you are struggling well.

Put it Down

Traveling steadily along God's path also means making conscious decisions to follow the ways of God. Struggling well involves obedience. Joseph put aside personal desire and ran away from Potiphar's wife. He made a decision to obey God. Joseph ran Potiphar's household well. He gave the task all his effort. Sure, he didn't want to be there. He didn't consider Egypt home. He didn't love his job. But he served faithfully. He was obedient.

We live in a world of self-indulgence. Every day you are invited to please and pamper yourself. You're told how difficult you have it and how you deserve so much more. You're encouraged to think of yourself first, to experience pleasure right now, and to forget what everyone else needs so you can take care of you. Our culture tells you that the goal of your life is to be happy—and the way to happiness is to serve yourself.

It's not popular to talk about obedience. It sounds so restrictive, so suffocating. To obey has become the opposite of fun and fulfillment.

Even Christians can get nervous when obedience talk starts. Believers become fearful that an emphasis on obedience to Jesus will compromise the grace of Jesus. There is a fear that a focus on obedience will drain our faith dry and send us spinning into works righteousness and the worship of self.

We've complicated and corrupted the simple teaching of Biblical obedience. As a consequence, we have created paralyzed followers of Jesus who hear the siren call of the culture more clearly than the sweet invitation of Christ.

Obedience, however, is not an empty void of joylessness and oppression that takes away everything good. It is an active and creative fullness. It is doing something meaningful to bring life and light to a dead and dark world. One of the words used for "obey" in the Old Testament is a word that means "to do" and "to make." A refrain about obedience repeated over and over in the Old Testament is, *"For the man who obeys [God's decrees and laws] will live by them" (Leviticus 18:5).* Obedience means life. If obedience disappears, arrogance, stubbornness, sin, and death take over. Obedience brings God's gift of life and light to a dying and empty world. Isaiah 50:10 says it well: *"Who among you fears the LORD and obeys the word of his servant? Let him who walks in the dark, who has no light, trust in the name of the LORD and rely on his God."* Obedience changes things. It is all about total reliance on God. It is living out trust in His work, not your own. It is implementing and doing what God gives you to do instead of running around in your own emptiness. Obedience doesn't take away. It adds.

Another word used for "obey" in the Old and New Testaments is a word that means "to keep" and "to hold on to." In

67

John 14:21 Jesus said, *"Whoever has my commands and obeys them, he is the one who loves me. He who loves me will be loved by my Father, and I too will love him and show myself to him."* When you hold onto God's gifts, you let go of what is crippling and poisoning your life. Instead of hanging onto that which destroys, you get to hold onto the transformational grace of God in Jesus Christ. God places something new into your hand. Obedience means holding onto that precious gift and seeing it change your life.

Moses experienced this life-renewing obedience. After he was called by God to free the people of Israel from slavery, Moses responded with some hesitation. In Exodus 4:1 Moses said to God, *"What if they do not believe me or listen to me and say, 'The LORD did not appear to you'?"* He was scared. He had a past. He had baggage. Verse two goes on: *"Then the LORD said to him, 'What is that in your hand?' 'A staff,' he replied."*

You see, Moses was holding on to his deepest wounds and failures. After he killed a man in Egypt and had two of his own countrymen make the act public, Moses ran away. He fled to a barren and desolate land to hide there as a shepherd. And he stayed for decades. By the time God called Moses to deliver the people from Egypt, he was eighty-years-old. He had been hanging on to his fear, depression, wounds, and failure since he was a strapping young man who lived in Pharaoh's household. Now he was being called to go back. God knew Moses needed something better than what he was holding on to. So the Lord looked at that shepherd's staff and told Moses, *"Throw it on the ground."*

Obedience, first, meant that Moses had to let go of his junk. It was ruining his life. Moses couldn't let go by himself. He

68

never would have done it. He liked his junk. He was comfortable with it. It was the way he was used to living—in barrenness, in hiding, in regret, and in fear. He was accustomed to it. So God gave him a new option: *"Throw it on the ground."* What happened next? *"Moses threw it on the ground and it became a snake, and he ran from it."*

God showed Moses the real nature of what he was holding onto. It was evil. It was rebellion. It was sucking life out of him.

Traveling steadily along God's path means putting down the junk you're holding onto. Is it pride? Is it an attitude of entitlement? Is it hidden sin? Is it a self-critical spirit? What junk are you clutching that you believe is giving you life? Jesus died to take it from your gnarled fist, expose it for what it is, and crush it. Jesus rose from death to give you something new to hold onto.

As the snake slithered in front of Moses, God commanded Moses to pick it back up. With fear and trembling, Moses grabbed the snake by the tail and it became a staff again. Exodus 4:20 reveals that Moses was now holding something completely different: *"So Moses took his wife and sons, put them on a donkey and started back to Egypt. And he took the staff of God in his hand."* Moses' tool of avoidance and despair had become God's instrument of miraculous freedom and rescue. Moses had something new in his hands. It was new life. It was a total change. It was redemption, the gift of God.

Obedience is hanging on to what God has given you. It is keeping the gift. Empowered by the Holy Spirit, it is living life with a miracle of restoration and transformation in your hands. It is carrying the "staff of God" into the world. Or, as Augustus

Toplady, author of the hymn "Rock of Ages" said, "Nothing in my hand I bring, only to Thy cross I cling." God's gift is in our hands for new life. The Bible summarizes it well in Romans 6:4, *"We were therefore buried with him through baptism into death in order that, just as Christ was raised from the dead through the glory of the Father, we too may live a new life."* Obedience flows from the gift of life in Christ.

Will you throw down the "staff" of your past? Will you let go of what interferes with a steady walk with God? Will you put it down and see the "staff of God" placed in your hand? Will you travel steadily along God's path, do what He is calling you to do, live the way He has redeemed you to live, and, as you hit the wall of struggle, struggle well?

Running With Horses

When I was a seminary student, one of my professors preached on Jeremiah 12:5. With a booming voice he shouted to the students, *"If you have raced with men on foot and they have worn you out, how can you compete with horses?"* His point was that if the ordinary trials and obstacles of life wore us down, how would we survive the holy calling, the difficult challenge, of serving Jesus? It was a stirring message. I never forgot it. When problems hit, I said to myself, "This can't conquer me. I have to run with horses!"

During a particularly low point of struggle, I went on a run during some vacation time. About halfway through the run, as I prayed and agonized about my angst and trouble, I saw horseshoe prints in the sandy soil. The sermon came back to me. "Wait a minute," I thought, "as I endure struggles, I need to keep putting one foot in front of the other. I need to trust Jesus and be faithful to

Him. I need to struggle well. After all, God will sustain me. He will give me strength to run with horses!"

The hoof prints were encouraging to me. I chuckled at God's reminder and at His sense of humor. I continued to pray and run. As I prayed, I grew in hope and strength. God's Word came back to me. I could wait upon Him. Even when I couldn't see it, God was working for me behind the scenes. His faithfulness would prevail. I was privileged to participate in the sufferings of Jesus. Nothing would separate me from His love. His promises are true and dependable.

That's when I saw the horses. I couldn't believe it. I rounded a corner and there before me were two horses with riders on the path ahead of me. I ran toward them, climbing a hill. They were sauntering at a slow pace, so I actually passed them up. As I ran past the horses, I nearly laughed out loud. Look at what God had done! Not only was I racing with men on foot, but I was racing horses and passing them! This, I thought, is what God can do. This is His power over adversity. This is His promise of victory. This was His statement of where I stood. As His beloved child, I was competing with horses! What struggle could ever really win?

If you are struggling, traveling steadily along God's path is your first course of action. On that path, you will not merely survive. You will not merely race with men on foot. You will run with horses!

Study Guide for Chapter 3:
Struggle Well by Traveling Steadily

1. How do you typically respond when your weaknesses and failures are exposed?

2. Read Psalm 41:1-2. What is God's attitude toward people who experience weakness?

3. How does God's perspective make it safe for Him to see your vulnerabilities and flaws?

4. If you have experienced dashed dreams, what has helped you keep going after your hopes crumbled?

5. The first step in handling dashed dreams is to do nothing. What might you feel like doing instead of waiting on God?

6. Read Romans 3:23-24. What truths about yourself are not easy for you to accept?

7. Read 1 Peter 2:9-10. How do these verses encourage you as you face yourself honestly?

8. In what areas of life do you need to travel steadily these days?

9. What strong feelings do you fight along this course?

10. How is God shaping you into a "crock-pot" believer and an obedient follower as you face your struggles?

Chapter Four
Struggle Well
with Worry Replacement

"Therefore do not worry about tomorrow, for tomorrow will worry about itself. Each day has enough trouble of its own."
Matthew 6:34

"I urge you, brothers, by our Lord Jesus Christ and by the love of the Spirit, to join me in my struggle by praying to God for me."
Romans 15:30

Crippling Worry

In the early 1990's my wife and I were participating in a "Through the Bible in a Year" program at our church. We were starting a building program and the congregation decided that, in addition to building buildings, they wanted to grow in their walk with Jesus, too. It was a great idea. So we made "One Year Bibles" available, we publicized the readings, and we encouraged everyone to participate in reading a portion of the Old Testament, a portion of the New Testament, part of the Psalms, and part of the book of Proverbs every day. That would bring us through the entire Bible in a year's time.

I'll never forget the day I came home at the beginning of this Bible reading effort and my wife said to me, "I've found my verse. This is the verse I need." It was Matthew 6:34, *"Therefore do not worry about tomorrow, for tomorrow will worry about itself. Each day has enough trouble of its own."* When she told me, I understood exactly why she needed this verse.

You see, ten years before this point in time we were a newly married couple. We just moved to St. Louis, and we had the worries that typical newly married couples have. Our "Worries in Life" list looked like this:

Money – We moved to St. Louis right out of college. We had little or no savings, so money was a big issue. We needed some.

Job – My wife was a new teacher. As a wife of a seminary student, she was competing with many other teachers to find a job in the St. Louis area. I had to get a job, too, if we were going to make ends meet in our new location. Jobs were major concerns.

Transportation – We had a one small used car. If any major repair was needed, we'd be done for.

The Future – What would the future hold for us? Would our health be okay? Would my schooling go well? Would we be able to start a family one day? We had worries about the future.

Ten years later life was much different. We had two small children, a big mortgage, and I was pastor of a church. Things had become a bit more complicated. In fact, our worry list went from the four categories above to something like THIS:

Safe delivery of kids – Illness – Diapers – Diaper rash – Formula – Solid food – Nursing – Sleeping through the night – Allergies – Doctors – Immunizations – Hospital bills – Ear infections – Congestion – Pink eye – Falling down stairs – Swallowing objects – Safe paint – Safe cabinets – Tub safety – Outdoor safety – Crossing the street – Skinned knees – Responsible babysitters – Stranger danger – Nice friends – Good education – Scouting opportunities – Sports opportunities – Good teachers – School system – Obeying rules – Bicycle safety – Tying shoes – Trick-or-treat safety – Getting spoiled – Not feeling left out – Obesity – Eating disorders – College tuition – Health plan – Vision testing – Hearing tests – Dating – Drugs – Alcohol – Peer Pressure – MySpace – Graces – ACT scores – SAT scores – College admission - Class rank – Summer activities – Driving – Insurance – TV shows – Movies – Cell phones – Text messages – Computer needs – Curfew – Bedtime – Church attendance – Bills – Homework – Projects – Having time together – Getting up on time – Vitamins – Junk food – Clothes – Sex – AIDS – Confirmation – Sunday School – Career plans – Marriage – Spouse – Faith – Criminals – Accidents – Pets – Wills – Godparents – Beneficiary designations

If you actually made it through the whole list without resorting to skimming, you probably noticed that this was just the worry list about kids! All of our worries couldn't fit into four neat categories anymore. The worries rushed in like giant waves crashing onto the shore of our lives. Life was hectic, messy, crazy, and overwhelming. So, when my wife said that she needed Matthew 6:34, I understood completely.

Every day, long lists of worries crash into your life. Worry after worry sends you running. The word Jesus used for "worry" in Matthew 6:34 has as its root a word that means "to divide" or "to distribute." Worry shatters your life into pieces and sends your heart and mind running in many different directions. You know how it feels. You have a fear of the unknown. You think about all the possible outcomes. You turn the scenarios over in your mind. You imagine what might take place. You even start to feel the emotions that all the dreadful possibilities bring. You become gripped by sadness, fear, panic, or despondency. Worry fractures your life, fragments your soul, and frazzles your nerves. Your life is sent on a wild ride.

> *Worry sends you running after all the things that might happen. It drains life from you as you enter the chase.*

Jesus even spoke about worry in terms of a chase. In Matthew 6:31-32 He said, *"So do not worry, saying, 'What shall we eat?' or 'What shall we drink?' or 'What shall we wear?' For the pagans run after all these things..."* Worry sends you running after all the things that might happen. It drains life from you as you enter the chase. When Jesus used the word "pagans," he was referring to what the world offers. Everything in the world is temporary. Its ultimate meaning is empty. The normal course of action in the world is a fruitless chase that drains life from you. And when you enter this chase, when you succumb to worry, you end up losing what's important to you.

When our family moved into our house in the early 1990's, we discovered that we lived in a neighborhood of dog comedy. At least once each week, neighborhood dogs would escape from their masters. It became a common occurrence to see a dog running down the street with an owner giving chase not far behind. My 6'7" Norwegian neighbor had a big Airedale. Every week we would look out our front window and see the dog run by. About ten seconds later my neighbor would follow, calling the dog's name and giving chase with arms waving. It was hilarious!

A family across the street had Afghans that would get loose—and I'm not talking blankets. The dogs loved a good break for freedom. They flopped out of the house if the door opened too widely and took off. Sometimes we would get involved in the chase, helping to catch a dog or letting the owners know which direction their pets ran.

One day, while my wife stood in the driveway after coming back from a bike ride, a Labrador ran by. Not long after that, its owner came huffing and puffing along. He paused at the end of our driveway and said hello. As he looked up and saw my wife's bicycle, you could almost see the light bulb go on over his head.

He said to my wife, "Do you think I could borrow your bike so I could catch my dog?"

Having grown up in the Chicago area, I learned one cardinal rule of bike riding: never give your bike to a stranger! But this man was very persuasive and my wife is very compassionate. The man, whom we had never met before, offered to give my wife his driver's license. He told her where he lived. He made a strong case and my wife relented. She lent him her bike.

About two hours after this episode I returned home and saw that my wife had one of the saddest expressions I had ever seen. She told me the whole story. When she got to the part about the man asking for the bike I thought to myself, "She didn't give him the bike. She couldn't have." But she did. What made it even sadder was that the bike was brand new—a gift I had given her earlier in the year. Now, after two hours, the bike was still gone. We didn't have his driver's license, but the man did give a general description of where he lived. I drove over to his area and found the bike lying on its side next to the road. I loaded it into the car and brought it home.

The point is: when you enter a chase—even with good intentions, you may end up losing what is important to you. When you enter the chase of worry—even for a good cause and with a compassionate heart, you may lose what is precious and life-giving. You may lose peace. You may lose contentment. You may lose a relationship because of your worry. You may lose the ability to use your talents as worry paralyzes you. You may even lose your trust in God.

Worry is destructive. It will drain life from you, sending you on a chase after what you cannot control, causing you to lose what is most important.

The Truth About Tomorrow
That's why Jesus said, *"Therefore do not worry about tomorrow, for tomorrow will worry about itself. Each day has enough trouble of its own."*

Some scholars have examined this verse and said that Jesus was being very philosophical. He was sounding like a typical Eastern teacher who spoke wise words to his followers. I don't agree. I am not convinced that Jesus was acting like a typical Eastern sage as He spoke these words. In fact, I see Jesus displaying His true nature as the Eternal Son of God in these words. I believe that Jesus was doing two things in this verse. First, He was telling the truth about tomorrow. Second, He was giving you a tool so you can face tomorrow.

In Matthew 6:34 Jesus did what you could never do. When He said, *"Each day has enough trouble of its own,"* He was looking at tomorrow. He was peering into the future for you. The verdict? Jesus saw that tomorrow has another wave of worries waiting for you. It has plenty of trouble. That word for "trouble" in this verse can also be translated as "evil." Jesus had a complete grasp of the sinful and broken world in which you live. He understood that you cannot simply place your hope in tomorrow. You need to place your hope in the Lord of tomorrow. Tomorrow will let you down. You can't simply sing the song from the musical "Annie": "Tomorrow, tomorrow, I love you tomorrow; you're only a day away!" Life will not get better all by itself.

That's why Jesus came to this earth to give His life on the cross and rise again from the grave. We needed His help. We needed a new way—a new approach to tomorrow. So the Savior died to conquer anything tomorrow will throw at you. In your collapsed condition from your aimless chasing, Jesus picked you up like a lost bike on the side of the road and brought you home. The new truth about tomorrow is that you have a future. You're forgiven. You have hope forever. And you have hope right now.

Only in a relationship with Jesus Christ do you have hope that withstands the waves of worry that crash into your life. Jesus gives you a precious gift: His blood-bought truth about tomorrow.

A Tool to Face Tomorrow: Worry Replacement

Jesus also gives you a tool to allow you to face tomorrow. He said in Matthew 6:33: *"Seek first his kingdom and his righteousness…"* As waves of worry pound you, you don't have to chase after the remedies of the world. You can seek the kingdom of God and His righteousness.

When the Bible talks about God's kingdom, it isn't referring to a building or a location. It means the way God operates, His way of doing things. The "righteousness of God" refers to the right way of God that culminates in salvation through Jesus. The Bible calls Jesus "the righteousness" of God (Jeremiah 23:6; 1 Corinthians 1:30). Through the saving work of Jesus, God has opened a new way of life—even a new way to face worry.

His new way to face worry is something I call Worry Replacement. It is a precious tool to face tomorrow. It's the key to struggling well when waves of worry hit. Worry Replacement means that when worry comes crashing in and starts to drain life from you, God gives you something better and life-giving to take its place.

The tactic we usually use to face worry is resistance. It's our gut reaction to trial, temptation, sadness and despair. We resist it. We try NOT to do something, feel something, or think about something. We attempt to push it away so we can keep it out of our lives and guard our hearts and minds from the invasion of that which makes us crumble and fail.

Self-control is laudable, but do you see the problem? Even if resistance is successful, there may not be anything to fill the void after you've repelled the assault. You may be able to keep worry away, but what do you do next? Is your only option to keep resisting?

Jesus addressed this issue when He spoke about the wicked generation of His day. He compared His listeners to a person who had an evil spirit driven out of him, but had nothing to fill up the empty space. It was a dangerous situation. Jesus said, *"Then [the evil spirit] says, 'I will return to the house I left.' When it arrives, it finds the house unoccupied, swept clean and put in order. Then it goes and takes with it seven other spirits more wicked than itself, and they go in and live there. And the final condition of that man is worse than the first"* *(Matthew 12:44-45).*

> *If you have a lot to resist but have nothing to fill you, big trouble can result. Something will always try to occupy your emptiness.*

If you have a lot to resist but have nothing to fill you, big trouble can result. Something will always try to occupy your emptiness. The devil, the world and our flesh are all about filling you with things that are not from God. So, along with NOT worrying, Jesus called you to SEEK His Kingdom. He REPLACED worry with Kingdom action. He provided a new pathway in life that allows you not merely to endure struggle, but to struggle well.

When I lived in the Chicago area, a friend of mine invited me to visit his running store. He owned a place called Running

Unlimited. I got to know him and his family at a Christian basketball camp we held every summer. One day I was talking with him about running and mentioned that I was having trouble finding my preferred brand of shoes. He told me about his business and invited me to stop by. I hesitated for a while because running stores can be expensive. I was more of the find-your-shoes-for-a-discount guy. But it got to the point that I finally had to give in. I needed new shoes desperately. Running shoes only last for 400-500 miles. After that point you need shoes that have new cushion and unworn tread. If you don't get new shoes, you'll end up with an injury. I was starting to ache, so I knew I had to go to the store. It was a great place. My friend found a new brand of shoes that was just right for my running needs. He let me test the shoes out. He even gave me a discount! Then he invited me to come back when I needed shoes again.

After 400-500 more miles, guess what I did? I went back. I returned to the store. Once again I got new cushion, unworn tread—and a discount! Again, he invited me back. When 400-500 miles passed, what did I do? I returned again, and again, and again. I was grateful. I was thrilled that I could return. When it was time to move to Texas, I went to the store to buy one last pair of shoes and to say goodbye to my friend. I told him that I wished I could come back even when I was in San Antonio, but after all these years it was time to say goodbye. Do you know what he said to me? He said, "Mike, you can buy your shoes from me online!" So I bought my shoes from his online store. I returned once again.

That's what Jesus was talking about when He said, *"Seek first the kingdom of God and his righteousness"* and *"do not worry."* He was making the point that life wears down your tread and takes your cushion away. If you keep on going for too long, if you keep on trying to hold out on your own, you're going to get hurt. So your Savior invites you not only to resistance, but to replacement. He brings you back, reconditions your soul (pun intended), and even gives you a discount on the whole thing! This new life is a gift. Then God looks you in the eye and invites you to come back again, and again, and again.

What did God do after spending six days creating the earth? He rested. After God's people were freed from brutal slavery in Egypt, what did God give them? He said, *"Remember the Sabbath day by keeping it holy. Six days you shall labor and do all your work, but on the seventh you are to rest."* God was saying, "No more worn tread. No more cushionless life. No more injuries from overuse. I am bringing you back for restoration. I am freeing you from slavery and replacing your emptiness with my gifts that restore your lives."

Are you so busy resisting that you have no opportunity for replacement? There's a rhythm of life these days that empties you out but doesn't fill you up. It's the drumbeat of constant activity. It's the non-stop, driving rhythm of relentless tragedy and pain. It's the pounding cadence of pressure to do more, to get things done, to try to catch up, and to try to keep up. It keeps going, pushing, pounding, never letting up. It's the rhythm of sin, of a broken life and world, of slavery to hopelessness. That's why life doesn't get better naturally. The devil will tell you that everything will be fine if you keep trying harder, if you stay awake at night to figure it all out, and if you keep pushing yourself and pushing all the bad stuff away. But the devil is lying. The natural rhythm of life is the rhythm of sin and decay, the rhythm of weariness and powerlessness. Do you feel it in your life? It's hard to miss, isn't it?

We need something new. We need something to fill the void. We need something to anchor us as waves of worry crash into our lives. What is it? It's another rhythm. It starts with a steady pounding sound, the pounding of nails and the pounding of the heart of God. Then the hammer stops. And the pounding of Jesus' heart slows. And stops. Then, silence. This rhythm happened on the cross. What took place there? Jesus broke the rhythm of sin and death. He broke the pattern of rest-lessness and decay in your life. God's love and forgiveness through Jesus Christ re-set the rhythm of your life.

Even though you are swamped with worry every day, Jesus dwells in you as the Rock of Salvation. The Old Testament didn't say that God was like a rock. It said that God IS a rock—our rock (Psalm 95:1). The word for "glory" in the Old Testament is a word that means "heavy." God's glory is heavy, weighty, and substantive. He is the One who dwells in you and holds you firm as the waves of worry pummel your life. You're not only tied to the Rock; you've got the Rock in you through all storm and struggle. He keeps bringing you back to Himself to fill you up, to give you new cushion, and provide fresh tread for the difficult race of life. He replaces your emptiness with the fullness of His presence.

When my daughters were very young we used to walk to a little park around the corner from our house. As my children began to grow up, they got to a point when they wanted to play all by themselves. So my wife and I would sit on a bench located in front of all the playground toys. The girls would climb and swing and slide. But every few minutes they would have to come tromping over the gravel-covered playground back to mom and dad. "Did you see me slide?" "Are you watching me?" "Can you brush me off?" Those are the things they would say. They kept coming back. Why? To know they weren't alone. To be encouraged. To get a little repair work done.

That's the gift God gives you. He blesses you with a tool to face tomorrow. He replaces your worry with good gifts. 1 Peter 2:24-25 says it so well, *"[Jesus] himself bore our sins in his body on the [cross];...by his wounds you have been healed. For you were like sheep going astray, but now you have returned to the Shepherd and Overseer of your souls."* God gives you something to fill the nothingness in life. He replaces resistance with wholeness and hope.

Struggle Well with Worry Replacement

What does worry replacement look like? Let's start with **prayer**. Psalm 55:22 says, *"Cast your cares on the Lord and he will sustain you..."* The word for "cares" is the same word Jesus used for "worry" in Matthew chapter 6. Prayer is a replacement for worry in your life. Philippians 4:6 tells us, *"Do not be anxious about anything, but in everything, by prayer and petition, with thanksgiving, present your requests to God."* The word for "anxious" is the same word Jesus used for "worry" in Matthew 6. You see a trend here, don't you? God's Word gives the gift of prayer as a worry replacement tool.

If anyone should have been a worry-wart, it would have been Abraham. God said to him in Genesis 12:1, *"Leave your country, your people and your father's household and go to the land I will show you."* That's it. Leave. Go away from family,

87

home, security, your neighborhood, everything. "Head into the wilderness. I'll show you where you'll end up."

What if that happened to you? Wouldn't it be nerve-wracking? Packing would be a nightmare in itself!

Of course, God gave Abraham a beautiful promise. God said, *"I will make you into a great nation and I will bless you; I will make your name great, and you will be a blessing. I will bless those who bless you, and whoever curses you I will curse; and all peoples on earth will be blessed through you" (12:2-3).* That was really good news, but Abraham still was called to go. How did he handle the dramatic change and deep uncertainty in his life?

> *Instead of objecting, speculating, complaining, and worrying, Abraham stopped to pray.*

Instead of getting stuck in worry, Abraham stopped to pray.

As Abraham approached the land of Canaan, God appeared to him again and told him that the land would be his one day. It was another great promise, but there were some very rough and threatening people living there. How would Abraham ever occupy that land one day? The promise could have caused even more worry and fretting. What did Abraham do? Instead of objecting, speculating, complaining, and worrying, Abraham stopped to pray. Genesis 12:7 says, that Abraham *"built an altar there to the LORD, who had appeared to him."* God showed

Abraham that prayer, conversation with God, replaced fear and worry.

If you keep reading about Abraham's life, you'll see that he ran into plenty of trouble. He made some bad decisions. He experienced some success. But through it all, he stopped to pray. When the land was getting too crowded for Abraham and his nephew to graze their herds together, as complication and complexity grew in Abraham's life, what did he do? He went back to the place where God appeared to him. What did he do there? Genesis 13:4 tells us that Abraham *"called on the name of the LORD."* Prayer replaced stress and worry.

After Abraham ventured into his new acreage and saw that it wasn't as user-friendly as he had hoped, what was his response? Worry loomed. Distress was knocking at the door. Fear was pressing upon him. Genesis 13:18 tells us, *"Abram moved his tents and went to live near the great trees of Mamre at Hebron, where he built an altar to the LORD."* Abraham prayed. Prayer was an active, powerful replacement for the emptiness of worry.

I've seen this in my life in wonderful ways. Over the years, our waves of worry have been replaced with prayer. My wife is a shy person—not the up front, pray aloud type. But I have seen her prayer life grow—and our prayer life together grow. As the worries of life have swept in, we have increased our prayer as a couple. Every night, before we go to sleep, we pray together. We've taught our children to pray. We encourage them to pray when times are difficult. When worries are rushing in, I've even heard my wife say as she walks through the house, "Dear Jesus, help us with this situation." Right then and there she replaces worry with prayer.

Prayer is a precious gift from God. I believe it is the primary worry replacement tool in the Bible. When Jesus was concerned about which disciples to choose, He stayed up all night praying. When Jesus faced the most anxiety-filled moment of His life in the Garden of Gethsemane—so stressful that His sweat was mingled with blood—He prayed. When Jesus hung on the cross, carrying the sins of the world, He prayed. Prayer pushes your worries to the sidelines of life and connects you with your Savior, His help, and His hope. It's worry replacement.

Will you make the conscious decision to pray instead of worry? When worry comes crashing in, when stress levels ramp up, when you're starting to feel frantic, instead of spinning out of control or wilting under the pressure, will you pray? Instead of lashing out or getting crazy within, will you talk to God? Instead of running around in a panic, will you fall on your knees in prayer? You struggle well in the midst of life-crushing worry when you replace worry with prayer. God hears you. He will respond. You're seeking first the Kingdom of God and his Righteousness. When you do that, Jesus promised that God will provide. He will step in.

A second worry replacement tool is **the Bible**. At a visit to Mary and Martha's house, as Martha worried frantically about all the arrangements, Jesus ended up saying to Martha, *"Martha, you are worried and upset about many things, but only one thing is needed" (Luke 10:41).* The "one thing needed" was to sit at the feet of Jesus and hear His Word. God's Word would replace the wild worry that filled Martha's heart and soul.

God's Word is a precious gift that has replaced worry throughout the ages. We talked about the trials and struggles of

90

Daniel earlier in this book. Daniel had every reason to wake up every morning with worry. The whims of crazy kings and the ill will of enemies took Daniel on a wild ride of unpredictability each day. What did Daniel do? In addition to regular and relentless prayer, he read the Bible. He held on to God's Word with tenacious desperation to replace the waves of daily worry that threatened to drown him.

Daniel 9:2-3 gives us a glimpse of how Daniel struggled well: *"In the first year of [Darius'] reign, I, Daniel, understood from the Scriptures, according to the word of the LORD given to Jeremiah the prophet, that the desolation of Jerusalem would last seventy years. So I turned to the Lord God and pleaded with him in prayer and petition, in fasting, and in sackcloth and ashes."* Daniel was stressed out about his captivity and the displacement of his people. What did he do? He prayed and read the Bible. He searched the Scriptures. He hung onto God's Word. It was his guide, his lifeline, and his source of soul-refreshment.

As Daniel's captivity dragged on, God got even more dramatic in giving Daniel doses of His Word. In the book of Daniel, chapters 7-12, God gave Daniel visions. These visions happened throughout Daniel's life, through the reigns of three different kings. Daniel wrote these visions down for us to read in the Bible. What was the main point of these visions? Were they given to complicate Daniel's life with confusing mysteries? No. Aside from the beautiful meaning of these visions, their first purpose was to sustain Daniel over the long haul with a personal Word from God. During Daniel's worry and distress, God spoke.

And God still speaks. The Bible is God's voice in your life. God's Word is living and active. It is your lamp and light in darkness. It is cleansing water when you're caked with the muck of hurt and failure. It is sweet food when you need nourishment for your soul. It is more precious than silver and gold, giving you real riches when you crash in the poverty of pain. God's Word fills you with the hope of life so worry can't empty you with the fear of loss. The Bible leads you to struggle well when worry rushes in.

My wife has read the Bible for years. She knows a lot about it. But I've seen the Bible develop as a worry replacement tool in her life in a unique way. It all started when she told a friend about her new verse, Matthew 6:34. The friend was artistic and made a special sign with her verse on it. My wife put the sign in a prominent location at home so she could see it and be reminded of Jesus' words when worries started to rush in. My wife found other signs and cards with other verses and placed them around the house. The Word became a vivid reminder of God's faithfulness and accessible help during times of worry.

Then she took another step. She started to wear bracelets with Bible verses on them. When the worries grow, my wife looks at her bracelets and is reminded of God's presence, love and care. One bracelet says, *"Lo, I am with you always" (Matthew 28:20)*. Another says, *"As for me and my house, we will serve the Lord" (Joshua 24:15)*. Another says, *"For God so loved the world that He gave His one and only Son, that whoever believes in Him shall not perish but have eternal life" (John 3:16)*. A couple Christmases ago I bought one for her that says, *"Do not worry" (Matthew 6:34)*. With the Word of God very close, worries are replaced.

But wait, there's more! Worry replacement is something you can share with others. As my daughters grew into young

92

adults, life became much more complicated for them. Pressures, relationships, and responsibilities brought plenty of worry and trouble. When the waves came crashing in, my wife would say to them at strategic times, "Would you like to wear one of my bracelets?" Time and again they would say, "Yes." Throughout the day they would be able to glance at their wrist and see the promises and faithfulness of God. The Word of God is a gift that replaces worry. It leads you to struggle well.

Are you reading the Bible? Are you feasting on the bread of life? Are you taking advantage of the lifeline God has given for your heart and soul? The Bible is not just a book for church or the classroom. It is God speaking into your life. The Bible is not a task book that you have to work through in a certain amount of time. It is not an assignment to be completed. It is God's voice. It is His conversation with you. Reading the Word of God means slow and steady listening to the One who loves you. The Bible is God's powerful Word that will sustain you and change your life.

A third worry replacement tool is **witness**. Paul said to his friend Philemon, *"Be active in sharing your faith, so that you will have a full understanding of every good thing we have in Christ" (vs. 6).* Paul was letting his friend know that when you share your faith, you receive blessing, too.

In Psalm 73 a man named Asaph recounted his woes and worries. He was facing some very serious issues. He became discouraged. He almost gave up on his life of faith. What helped him with these brutal waves of worry? He said at the end of the Psalm, *"My flesh and my heart may fail, but God is the strength of my heart and my portion forever. Those who are far from you will perish; you destroy all who are unfaithful to you. But as for me, it is good to be near God. I have made the Sovereign LORD my refuge; I will tell of all your deeds."*

Telling about God's deeds replaced the oppressive pounding of the world. Remembering and proclaiming God's action brought confidence and hope to personal paralysis. Witness replaced worry.

I've seen it work. As I've sat with people whose lives are flooded with worry, I've heard them articulate the deeds of the Lord. Remembering what He has done, they were lifted out of worry to new confidence. By speaking about His deeds, they brought encouragement to the people around them.

> *Telling about God's deeds replaced the oppressive pounding of the world.*

Witness is not just for the courageous and bold. It is a worry replacement tool for the most quiet and timid people. I've seen gentle souls, shy as can be, share the hope and comfort of Jesus in ways that push worry out of the picture. I've heard people gently bring up the name of Jesus as they spoke to friends and family members about something that involved worry. Small statements of encouragement like "Jesus can help" or "I'll remember to ask Jesus about that" can be powerful words of witness. In cards and notes, I've seen faithful encouragers mention the name of Jesus. That's a powerful witness because, as the Bible says in Philippians 2:10, *"At the name of Jesus every knee shall bow, in heaven and on earth and under the earth."* Bringing Jesus into the picture pushes worry away. Worry cannot remain in the presence of Jesus! Witness is a tool for worry replacement. Witness is a tool to struggle well.

Will you remember the deeds of the Lord in your life? Will you tell of His deeds? Will you fill the gaps of fear and uncertainty with the grace of the Savior who has come to rescue us and walk with us? Will you tell your children the stories of God's grace in your life? Will you give Jesus credit for getting you as far as you've gotten? Will you speak the name of Jesus to replace the scourge of worry?

Take the Limo Home

Worry replacement is a tool that I need desperately. It is what I need to push worry away when it comes rushing in over and over again. It is the only way I can be filled with what is life-giving instead of that which is life-draining. Jesus addressed daily struggle in our lives when He said, *"Therefore do not worry about tomorrow, for tomorrow will worry about itself. Each day has enough trouble of its own."*

My question for you is: What about your life? When worry rushes in, will you struggle poorly or will you struggle well?

Several years ago we took a family vacation. It required a trip to the airport, so we called a limousine service to bring us there. That's pretty customary in Chicago. Many times it's cheaper and more reliable to get a limo instead of a cab. The car picked us up and brought us to the airport—it was a four-door sedan, nothing fancy. When we returned, I called the limo company and the person on the phone said, "Mr. Newman, I'm sorry, but we have a problem. Your car isn't available. We'll have to send a replacement." The person gave me the license number of the new car and we waited curbside for it to arrive.

Not too long after my phone call, a car pulled up. I checked the plate. I looked at it again. Then I turned to my wife and young daughters and said, "Look at the car they sent for us." It was a shining white stretch limousine! We climbed into the cavernous automobile and saw glimmering lights, long leather seats, a television, refreshments, and all kinds of luxuries. We told our daughters, "Don't touch anything!" And in silent awe we rode all the way home.

How will you live your life? Will you go home in the four-door sedan of worry, or will you ride in the shining stretch limousine of worry replacement—prayer, God's Word, and witness? Will you struggle with worry poorly or will you let God and His gift of new life lead you to struggle well?

Study Guide for Chapter 4:
Struggle Well with Worry Replacement

1. What are some of the big worries in your life right now?

2. How are these worries affecting you and the people in your life?

3. Read Matthew 6:25-30. What is Jesus saying to you in these verses?

4. How have you seen Jesus' faithful provision in your life?

5. How does this track record of your Savior help you handle worries?

6. Read Matthew 6:31-34. What did Jesus mean when He said to "seek first the kingdom of God"?

7. The first worry replacement tool mentioned in this chapter is prayer. Read Philippians 4:6-7. What does the Bible say about the benefit of prayer as you face worry?

8. The second worry replacement tool mentioned is the Bible. Read Psalm 119:103-107. How does God's Word help you when you face worry?

9. The third worry replacement tool mentioned is witness. Read Matthew 5:14-16. How does sharing God's faithful action in your life push worry away?

10. Brainstorm how you can grow stronger in your prayer life, your reading of the Bible, and in your witness for Jesus.

Chapter Five
Struggle Well
with Humble Forgiveness

———————

"He was despised and rejected by men, a man of sorrows, and
familiar with suffering...But he was pierced for our transgressions,
he was crushed for our iniquities; the punishment that brought us
peace was upon him, and by his wounds we are healed."
Isaiah 53:3, 5

"For our struggle is not against flesh and blood..."
Ephesians 6:12

Wounded

On January 8, 1993 two men waited until all the customers
had left a Brown's Chicken restaurant in Palatine, Illinois. The
details of what happened that night may never be fully known, but
the two men proceeded to kill the seven employees in the store that
evening. They took less than $2000 in cash.

In 2002 a break in the case allowed police to arrest the two
criminals. Both were found guilty and sentenced to life in prison.
But in the days, months, and years that followed the senseless
killings, the families of the victims were heartbroken, confused,
and angry.

I was part of a group of local clergy that helped minister to
the families and the community during that difficult time. Two of

the victims were high school students, attending the school just blocks from our church. Students and families throughout Palatine were shocked and frightened by such a brutal crime in their seemingly safe and relatively quiet suburb of Chicago.

One year after the crime, the families gathered in our church to remember their loved ones. I'll never forget speaking with the father of one of the high school boys who was killed. In his tears he said to me, "I must forgive whoever did this horrible thing, whoever took my son's life."

How could he forgive? As he suffered with a depth of emptiness, hurt, and loss that most people could barely comprehend, how could he speak words of forgiveness? For criminals—monsters—he didn't even know, how could he resolve to let this go?

Letting Go

Jesus had a lot to say about forgiving. In Matthew 6:12-15 Jesus included forgiving in the Lord's Prayer, emphasizing how important it is to forgive others:

> *"Forgive us our debts, as we also have forgiven our debtors. And lead us not into temptation, but deliver us from the evil one." For if you forgive men when they sin against you, your heavenly Father will also forgive you. But if you do not forgive men their sins, your Father will not forgive your sins.*

Forgiveness was a requirement. In Matthew chapter 18, Peter asked Jesus the famous question, *"Lord, how many times shall I forgive my brother when he sins against me? Up to seven* times?" Jesus answered, *"I tell you, not seven times, but seventy-seven times" (vss.21-22)*. Jesus then went on to tell the parable of the servant who didn't forgive even after his huge debt was forgiven by a compassionate king. Once again, Jesus emphasized extravagant forgiveness. After describing the unforgiving man's punishment, Jesus tacked on a warning at the end of the parable: *"This is how my heavenly Father will treat each of you unless you forgive your brother from your heart" (vs. 35)*.

How can anyone forgive so lavishly and generously—especially when it has to happen during the depths of hurt and pain? Jesus' disciples puzzled over this. Jesus said to them in Luke 17:3-4, *"So watch yourselves. If your brother sins, rebuke him, and if he repents, forgive him. If he sins against you seven times in a day, and seven times comes back to you and says, 'I repent,' forgive him."* The disciples were so stunned they replied, *"Increase our faith!" (vs.5)*

As Jesus suffered on the cross—unjustly, with torturous hate and ridicule hurled His way, He spoke words that run completely against the grain of what our normal response would be. He said about his killers, *"Father, forgive them, for they do not know what they are doing" (Luke 23:34)*. Then, after Jesus' resurrection, one of the first commissions He gave to His disciples was all about forgiveness: *"If you forgive anyone his sins, they are forgiven; if you do not forgive them, they are not forgiven" (John 20:23)*. Clearly, the forgiveness of others was a top priority for Jesus.

The Apostle Paul emphasized the need for believers to be people of forgiveness. He said in Ephesians 4:32, *"Be kind and compassionate to one another, forgiving each other, just as in*

101

Christ God forgave you." In Colossians 3:13 Paul writes, *"Bear with each other and forgive whatever grievances you may have against one another. Forgive as the Lord forgave you."* The word used for "forgive" in these verses from Paul's writing conveys the idea of giving a generous gift. A follower of Jesus was to have a hand that opened freely to contribute grace and pardon. After all, this is what God the Father did when He lavished His love upon us in Jesus. Another New Testament word for "forgive" means "to let go." God let go of our sins as He nailed them to the cross with His Son. He opened His hand of provision and mercy to give us a new reality of freedom and restoration, of a fresh start. Now we are called to forgive as He has forgiven us. But why? Why forgive? And, how? How can we be so generous to ones who hurt us so deeply?

Why Forgive?

I remember meeting a man who held onto grudges and hurts with a tight fist and hardened soul. He could remember every hurtful event, every cross word, and every injustice he ever suffered. He was quietly angry. Rage boiled below the surface of his calm exterior. But the results of unforgiveness seeped through every fissure of his being. He was not a happy man. His refusal to forgive could be seen physically. He walked hunched over and limping, as if a massive burden was on his shoulders. It was clear that all he held on to was crippling him. His family kept their distance from him and even suffered the effects of his bitter spirit. Not letting go was destroying him and everyone around him, slowly and completely.

Jesus knew that we need forgiveness—not only for our own redemption, but for our own survival and freedom. Jesus knew that forgiveness is an essential lifeline for each of us. Unforgiveness will destroy us.

Think about Jesus' teaching on forgiveness. While we often pay attention to the people who do the forgiving in the New Testament accounts that deal with reconciliation, the characters in the shadows of unforgiveness also teach us some stark lessons. In Matthew 18, the unforgiving servant ended up being put into prison and tortured because he refused to forgive a small debt (vs. 34). Matthew 20's first workers in the vineyard grumbled against their provider when they dove into resentment against the workers who had it easy (vs. 11). The Teachers of the Law in Mark 2 became bitter and accusatory after Jesus forgave the sins of the paralyzed man (vss. 6-7). As the sinful woman anointed Jesus' feet with perfume in Luke 7, Simon the Pharisee revealed his judgmental and loveless heart. After the prodigal son came home in Luke 15, the older son stood outside his father's house with a spirit steeped in comparison and resentment. With an unforgiving heart, he ruptured a precious relationship. In the parable of the Pharisee and the tax collector (Luke 18), Jesus showed the callous heart of an unforgiving person who had become completely self-absorbed and was drained of compassion. The episode of the woman caught in adultery in John chapter 8 shows how unforgiveness oozes out of corrupt souls in the form of violence and meanness.

The price of unforgiveness is high. It tortures and imprisons. It twists the soul into dark resentment and bitterness. It drains the heart of compassion and love. It severs relationships and drives you into lonely torment. It makes you mean and ready to explode with anger and hurt.

It is no wonder that Jesus emphasized the need, the calling, and the necessity to forgive and why the Scriptures teach forgiveness as an essential ingredient of life. Unforgiveness will make you miserable. It will take life from you. It will take you captive and lock you in a jaw-clenched, fear-filled, heart-worn dungeon.

Even worse, unforgiveness will foul up your relationship with God. Time and again we hear in the Bible that holding back forgiveness will do something to damage the way God reaches into your life. Jesus said in Mark 11:25, *"When you stand praying, if you hold anything against anyone, forgive him, so that your Father in heaven may forgive you your sins."* As He taught about prayer, Jesus said in Matthew 6:14-15, *"For if you forgive men when they sin against you, your heavenly Father will also forgive you. But if you do not forgive men their sins, your Father will not forgive your sins."*

> *Unforgiveness will make you miserable. It will take life from you. It will take you captive and lock you in a jaw-clenched, fear-filled, heart-worn dungeon.*

Something spiritually harmful happens when you fill up a reservoir of unforgiveness in your life. You get out of step with God. You stop reflecting His character. You nudge Him away and, in some way, clog the gracious conduit of God's grace into your life.

Contrast that with the effects of forgiveness. What relief, glee, and new life did the servant in Matthew 18 feel when the king forgave his million dollar debt? How delighted were the vineyard workers who received a full day's pay for one hour of labor? Can you imagine the spring in the step of the paralyzed man whose sins were forgiven and paralysis was healed? Can any of us quantify the love that overflowed from the heart of the forgiven woman as she poured perfume on Jesus' feet? Would the once-prodigal son ever be able to catch his breath after being welcomed home so extravagantly by his forgiving father? Would the forgiving father ever let the celebration end? What new lease on life did the woman caught in adultery have after Jesus sent her back into life forgiven? Can you imagine the power of forgiveness in the lives of the tax collectors, sinners, outcasts, and guilt-laden as Jesus forgave them?

Forgiveness results in freedom. It is fertile ground for love and compassion. It opens up new possibilities, changes attitudes and outlooks for the better, unleashes generosity, and creates souls overflowing with gratitude. Forgiveness tunes the soul to God's wavelength of purpose and redemption.

Do you remember how Joseph, son of Jacob, was victimized and violently cast aside? In Genesis chapter 45, Joseph revealed his identity to his brothers. It had been more than twenty years since Joseph was thrown into a pit and sold into slavery. Instead of holding on to unforgiveness, Joseph let the pain go. Eventually, he stood face to face with his brothers and verbalized his forgiveness:

> *Joseph said to his brothers, "I am Joseph! Is my father still living?" But his brothers were not able to answer him, because they were terrified at his presence. Then Joseph said to his brothers, "Come close to me." When*

they had done so, he said, "I am your brother Joseph, the one you sold into Egypt! And now, do not be distressed and do not be angry with yourselves for selling me here, because it was to save lives that God sent me ahead of you. For two years now there has been famine in the land, and for the next five years there will not be plowing and reaping. But God sent me ahead of you to preserve for you a remnant on earth and to save your lives by a great deliverance. So then, it was not you who sent me here, but God. He made me father to Pharaoh, lord of his entire household and ruler of all Egypt" (vss. 3-8).

Notice how Joseph the forgiver was free and joyful. He walked closely with God and was locked in on God's purpose. He was dialed in to hope and a promising future. He freed his imprisoned brothers from a life of guilt and shame. Later, he would promise to provide for his brothers and their families after their father died.

Forgiveness did something good and powerful for Joseph, his family, the entire population of Egypt, and the surrounding nations that were experiencing famine. Forgiveness unleashed results beyond what anyone could have predicted. That's the miraculous nature of forgiveness. The outcome is more than just the opposite of unforgiveness. Instead, the impact of forgiveness is exponential. It is positive, constructive, good, and life-changing. And God desperately wants it to be an active part of your life.

How to Forgive

But how? How could Joseph forgive? How could the parents of their murdered teenage son forgive? How can you forgive?

106

The question wouldn't be so difficult if everyone who ever hurt you approached you humbly, expressed sorrow for what they did, clearly articulated how they fouled up, and begged for forgiveness. That would make forgiveness much easier. Forgiving people who express sincere repentance—turning away from wrongdoing, expressing sorrow, and resolving to change their ways—is a journey that can be manageable and even joyful.

Cooperation in the process of forgiveness is the best possible scenario. When people see the error of their ways and seek to restore their relationships with you, you are helped along the way as you travel the road of forgiveness. Your heart is nurtured and restored when a hurtful person shows genuine sorrow. Doors of generous compassion can be opened in your heart when someone demonstrates true repentance.

But how can you forgive when the hurt is very deep and the perpetrator is cold and distant? How can you forgive when the person who injured you is absent—out of your life or, like the murderers of the seven victims in Palatine, unknown or inaccessible? How can you forgive when someone is determined to keep hurting you? How can you forgive if the other person doesn't care?

That's where the meaning of the word "forgive" comes into play. Remember, one of the key meanings of the word "forgive" means "to let go." When the ideal scenario of forgiveness doesn't pan out in your life, your lifeline becomes the ongoing action of letting go. You give the burden and pain to God.

Initially, this may sound like a cliché: Let go and let God. But it is far from cliché. It is an opportunity from God and a calling for all who hurt. The Bible says, *"Cast all your anxiety on him because he cares for you" (1 Peter 5:7).* Peter was quoting from the Bible, *Psalm 55:22, "Cast your cares on the LORD and he will sustain you; he will never let the righteous fall."* God calls His people to, literally, throw their worries and pain upon Him. Psalm 55 broadens the category of your burdens by letting you know that you can hurl everything upon the Lord—whatever it is. He wants you to let go, to give it to Him.

Jesus said, *"Come to me, all you who are weary and burdened, and I will give you rest. Take my yoke upon you and*

> *There are only two places for pain to dwell: inside yourself or in the body of the crucified Christ.*

learn from me, for I am gentle and humble in heart, and you will find rest for your souls" (Matthew 11:28-29). Jesus wants you to carry His light yoke of relief from burdens instead of the heavy yoke of your personal pain. In fact, Jesus came to carry that pain for you. Isaiah 53:4 says about the Savior, *"Surely he took up our infirmities and carried our sorrows."* Matthew 8:17 connected this prophecy to the casting out of demons and physical healing of people in desperate need. Jesus came to remove people's pain. On the cross He carried everything that causes you to die inside. There are only two places for pain to dwell: inside yourself or in the body of the crucified Christ. Your heart and mind will either be weighed down by hurt, injury, and brokenness, or Jesus can carry that heavy yoke. You must let it go. You have the gracious opportunity to let it go.

This is forgiveness in relationship with God. When you have no one to forgive, no one who wants to be forgiven, no one who will walk with you in the journey of reconciliation, you can practice forgiveness with God.

What does this forgiveness look like? How do you throw pain and hurt away? How do you cast brokenness upon the Savior?

It starts with simple conversation.

Struggle Well with Humble Forgiveness

The first conversation happens with God. This is where prayer life takes on new meaning—especially if you think of prayer as a formal, "churchy" ritual that only skilled pastors can do well, or that only happens before meals. In 1 Thessalonians 5:17, the Apostle Paul urges believers to *"pray continually."* Paul lets you know that prayer is the ongoing conversation you have with God—out loud and inside your head. Instead of bearing your own burdens, figuring out your own solutions, and hashing through your own hurts, you're called to bring everything to God in prayer—all the time.

This takes humility. You need to acknowledge that you cannot carry the load of everything in your life. You need to get to the point of admitting that you need help. You need to understand that you cannot bear the burden of your future, your past, or your present. It's all too big for you. But God can help.

In the context of solving conflict and relationship issues, James 4:10 says, *"Humble yourselves before the Lord, and he will lift you up."* Just before Peter reminded us to cast our cares on the

Lord, he said, *"Humble yourselves, therefore, under God's mighty hand, that he may lift you up in due time"(1 Peter 5:6).* With a humble attitude, you are invited to talk to God, asking for help and begging Him to carry the burden of your hurt and pain. Humble forgiveness starts with the continuous dialog of prayer, trusting that God can and will lift you up and show you the way.

That's how the father of the high school boy who was killed forgave the invisible and unknown killers. He prayed. He let go. In each moment of torturous pain, he begged God to carry the terrible burden. Every time hatred welled up in his soul, he asked God to take it away and replace it with healing and trust. When waves of sadness washed over him, he released his grief to God in prayer. This was not easy. It was an ongoing struggle, but the father knew that he could not carry this cauldron of emotions. It would destroy him. But God had shoulders big enough to handle it. In fact, Jesus carried this crushing hurt—in advance—on the cross. So the father handed it over. From moment to moment, heartbeat to heartbeat, agonizing day to endless night, he humbled himself before God and prayed.

And God came through. God carried the pain. It was still a struggle for the father. The pain would never disappear. But now he did not have to struggle alone. There was someone stronger carrying the load. The father understood David's words in Psalm 6:

> *I am worn out from groaning; all night long I flood my bed with weeping and drench my couch with tears. My eyes grow weak with sorrow; they fail because of all my foes. Away from me, all you who do evil, for the LORD has*

*heard my weeping. The LORD has heard my cry for
mercy; the LORD accepts my prayer (vss. 6-9).*

Giving your hurt to God in prayer, letting go of your pain
and allowing your caring heavenly father to bear your burden, is
essential to struggling well. This is a step of forgiveness that will
allow you to live as one freed from the enslaving chains of hatred
and resentment. It takes time. It requires practice and patience.
But it brings new life.

Too often, the hurt in your life dominates your thinking.
Your mind becomes overrun with anger, negativity, vengeance,
and your own problem-solving scenarios. When people hurt you,
your thought life can take a turn for the worse. You may start to
imagine what it would be like to yell at your enemy—to give it to
him or her with both barrels. You may construct eloquent speeches
that contain some serious verbal assaults. You may think of ways
to get revenge. You may strategize how you can make your
adversary suffer. Or you may wrack your brains to figure out
solutions and plans to fix the problem.

This swirl of ideas courses through your brain,
commandeers your thoughts, and makes you more miserable than
ever. Your constant brooding leads you to become steeped in
negativity or frustration. Anger boils below the surface of your
fragile exterior as you review the hurt over and over and over
again. Slowly, you become a slave to the person who hurt you.
Your life is dominated by the pain they inflicted. The person you
really are becomes lost. Instead, you travel aimlessly down a road
of bitterness and ugly negativity. You're mad at others, yourself,
and God. It's a miserable way to live. You need to let go. You
need to give it to God. You need to forgive steadily and humbly.

111

After a very difficult time in my ministry, I remember asking God to carry the burden of my hurt. I needed healing and restoration from wounds that left me tired, uncertain about continuing in ministry, and afraid to trust people in the church. After trying to take care of it myself, I realized that I could not come up with the solutions. I could never navigate my way through the deep hurt I felt. So I prayed. I kept praying. During that season of life I wrote out my prayers. I wanted to empty my system of the pain and see how God would respond. It took time, but God healed the pain. It actually took ten years—ten years!— before my stomach wouldn't feel the nervous jitters of dread when the ugly and hurtful years of ministry came up in conversation. God brought healing. He carried the burden, allowed me to grow and rediscover myself, and removed the pain.

During a time of life when some people close to me were testing me to the limit and causing some deep hurt in my heart, I remember my morning runs turning into morning rants. As I ran, I began to think terrible thoughts. I started to imagine what harsh words I would say to those scoundrels. In my mind, I gave them what they deserved. I tried to figure out subtle and clever ways I could get back at them and make them suffer. Those no-good people were going to pay! With each step I became more angry and more miserable. But I realized I was falling into a pit of unforgiveness. My morning jogs were always times of prayer, but in this pain they were turning into tirades of talk that was anything but godly. My thought life was getting out of control and taking me down a destructive path. I realized that I had to turn my negative and hateful thoughts into prayers for help. So, every time name-calling started to dominate my thoughts, I started to speak a prayer of blessing for the people who hurt me. I asked God to help them and reach them in a way that I couldn't. Every time I started to try to figure out how I could control the situation, I asked God, instead, to show me His way and come up with ideas that I could never imagine. Every time I descended into self-pity and a "woe is me" spirit, I told my Heavenly Father that I trusted Him and would walk with Him as He solved the issue.

As you experience hurt and anger, your thought life can get out of control. The rage inside your head can poison every part of your being. Reining in your straying thoughts and entering into an ongoing conversation with God is essential to struggling well.

Forgiveness means letting go. The practice of humble forgiveness starts by handing your hatred and hurt to God in prayer. This constructive conversation will free you from the crippling and self-destructive effects of unforgiveness. From moment to moment and day to day, you can give the burden of your pain to God.

> *Struggling well in relationships means that you willingly and humbly say you're sorry.*

Practicing Repentance

But there's more. Humility means that you are also willing to admit your own wrongs. You not only get hurt in life; you also hurt other people. Intentionally or unintentionally, you cause some pain in the hearts and souls of others. Struggling well in relationships means that you willingly and humbly say you're sorry. You confess your wrongs. You articulate how you hurt another person and you ask for forgiveness. You help drain away

113

the pain from another person's heart. You change your ways and show others that you will try your best not to hurt them again.

It is so tempting to start a fight instead of humbly repenting. It is so enticing to prove that you're right instead of working to salvage a relationship. It is so attractive to hold on to your way instead of letting go and giving in to show that you truly love someone. I'm not talking about compromising your ethical foundations or giving up you convictions. I'm talking about being quiet when your words aren't doing any good and trying someone else's way when your way is clearly causing problems.

How many conflicts have escalated into major battles because a husband refused to ask for directions or a wife wouldn't stop saying, "I told you so"? How many deep wounds have fractured relationships because a father or son wouldn't give in just a little bit? Stubbornness can turn a small disagreement into a "whale" of a problem.

Remember Jonah. He didn't see eye to eye with God when it came to reaching out to the evil and godless people in the city of Nineveh. Instead of obeying God, Jonah ran the opposite direction and boarded a boat that would take him far away from the problem. You remember the story. God sent a storm, Jonah was tossed overboard, and a big fish swallowed the fleeing prophet. From inside the fish, Jonah reconsidered his position. As the pain and darkness of his pride became real, Jonah realized that he needed to be humble before God. From the belly of the fish he prayed:

> *You hurled me into the deep, into the very heart of the seas, and the currents swirled about me; all your waves*

and breakers swept over me. I said, "I have been banished from your sight; yet I will look again toward your holy temple." To the roots of the mountains I sank down; the earth beneath barred me in forever. But you brought my life up from the pit, O LORD my God. When my life was ebbing away, I remembered you, LORD, and my prayer rose to you, to your holy temple. Those who cling to worthless idols forfeit the grace that could be theirs. But I, with a song of thanksgiving, will sacrifice to you. What I have vowed I will make good. Salvation comes from the LORD (Jonah 2:3-9).

Jonah recognized that he created a problem. His pride wreaked havoc in his life and in the lives of the people around him. As he sloshed around in the dark and acidic environment of a fish's stomach, He humbly acknowledged God as the One he needed to follow. Finally, he gave in and pledged that he would obey God.

What dark and acidic environment are you sloshing around in? Do you need to give in? Do you need to compromise? Do you need to say you're sorry? Do you need to let go of your pride and approach the other person in a loving and gentle way so a new beginning can take place?

After Jonah repented, God commanded the fish to vomit Jonah onto dry land. He didn't feel or smell very good at that point in his life. Humility is not always comfortable or pleasant. But it takes you out of darkness and puts you on God's path again. If you're in the mire of unforgiveness, I pray that your life will be turned inside out enough so that you will humbly repent. In that condition of willingness to follow God, I pray that He causes you to be spit out onto the dry ground so you can live again. How

115

might you need to let go of pride and start to struggle well by practicing repentance? It may be your time.

Forgiving and Forgetting

When I was growing up, I was made to say "I'm sorry" whether I liked it or not. You may remember the same thing: grudgingly shaking hands while you looked the other kid in the eyes. On the outside you were apologizing. On the inside you were thinking, "This is not the last of it. I'm gonna get you when the first chance comes around."

People say that you've got to forgive and forget, but is that realistic? The fact is, you DO remember that people hurt you. You're scarred and bruised. Must you really forget?

On one hand, the answer is no. Remembering helps you stay away from ongoing injury or abuse. It allows you to establish healthy boundaries. It teaches you what does and doesn't work in a relationship. You can't forget the lessons you learn in a healthy relationship, and you can't forget the important cautions you figure out when an unhealthy person is in your life.

Of course, there is unhealthy remembering. Grudges that fill you with growing hatred can't be allowed to linger in your life. Past hurts that rule your life and poison your attitude must be put behind you. Wounds that cripple you with fear need to, somehow, disappear from your consciousness.

Jonah provides a good case study in forgiving and forgetting—not because he was so good at it, but because he struggled with it just like we do. In Jonah chapter 4, the prophet was angry with God because God forgave and saved the evil

Ninevites. The lives of over 100,000 people were rescued, but what was Jonah's reaction? Chapter 4 begins:

> *But Jonah was greatly displeased and became angry. He prayed to the LORD, "O LORD, is this not what I said when I was still at home? That is why I was so quick to flee to Tarshish. I knew that you are a gracious and compassionate God, slow to anger and abounding in love, a God who relents from sending calamity. Now, O LORD, take away my life, for it is better for me to die than to live" (vss. 1-3).*

Jonah was ticked off that the unfaithful people of Nineveh got a second chance. He was angry and didn't shy away from telling God about it. Jonah expressed his emotion. He stated his grievance. He articulated his hurt.

In order to put hurt behind you, your hurt must be recognized and brought out into the open. You've got to express the emotion. That may mean venting to someone trustworthy and strong. It may involve processing the issue with a counselor or advisor. It could mean approaching the person who wronged you or whom you wronged to have a heart to heart discussion about the problem. It may mean talking to God if you're angry with Him or if you can't talk to the person who wounded you.

Your job is not to bury the pain you experience in life. Forgetting does not mean refusing to deal with issues. The first step in forgetting is to remember and to face the problem. God didn't ignore our sins. He dealt with them—every one of them—when He sent Jesus to die for them. It is so important to understand what you're feeling and to make sure you're not stuffing hurt away because it's too difficult to face.

After Jonah expressed the emotion, he listened and waited. Verses 4-5 tell us: *"But the LORD replied, 'Have you any right to be angry?' Jonah went out and sat down at a place east of the city. There he made himself a shelter, sat in its shade and waited to see what would happen to the city."*

Forgiving and forgetting takes time. It's a gradual process, not an instantaneous event. It's something you have to work at and let settle into your soul. It takes time to figure out what you're feeling and what your response should be. God helped this process by asking Jonah a good question. Did he have the right to be angry? Jonah had to search his heart to see if his anger was justified. Time will help you evaluate the appropriateness of your emotions.

Jonah also built a shelter. He had to find a location, gather the materials, and put it together. Once again, that took time. Jonah needed to sit, think, watch, and pray. Psalm 4:4-5 advises us to take this course when anger strikes: *"In your anger do not sin; when you are on your beds, search your hearts and be silent. Offer right sacrifices and trust in the LORD."* Before you can forget, you need to reflect. You need to settle down. You need to be quiet and spend some time with God. Forgiving and forgetting takes time.

Lewis Smedes, author of <u>Forgive and Forget</u>, said that your forgiveness should come not too soon and not too late. How do you know when that is? Jonah found out in the closing verses of chapter 4. God provided a vine to grow and shade Jonah as he thought about what God had done. As suddenly as the vine grew, it died. Jonah sat in the scorching sun and he wished he would die. That is when God spoke up:

> *But God said to Jonah, "Do you have a right to be angry about the vine?" "I do," he said. "I am angry enough to die." But the LORD said, "You have been concerned about this vine, though you did not tend it or make it grow. It sprang up overnight and died overnight. But Nineveh has more than a hundred and twenty thousand people who cannot tell their right hand from their left, and many cattle as well. Should I not be concerned about that great city?"*

God made it clear to Jonah that it was time to let go of his resentment. It was time to move on. As you watch and pray, God will let you know when it's time to let go of your hurt or anger. If you listen for His direction, God will show you when you can begin the process of forgetting. He will grow you and lead you on your journey of letting go. He will help you remember what you need to remember, allowing you to maintain healthy boundaries and making sure you don't become someone's doormat. And He will help you forget what you need to forget, purging the toxins of unforgiveness from your life. Slowly, your Savior God will help make you whole again.

Forgiving Yourself

Not long ago I was with a group of people who were discussing the issue of forgiveness. The group was asked what the greatest challenge of forgiveness was. I was surprised to hear how the majority of the group responded. The greatest challenge? Forgiving yourself.

119

It's so easy to be hard on yourself. You can cut others some slack. You can overlook the faults of the people around you. You can forgive the offenses of your loved ones and of strangers. But when it comes to your failures, your faults, and your foul-ups, you struggle to find any grace for yourself.

As I've gotten older, I see my failures with more clarity. I know where I've blown it as a parent. I see how I stumble as a husband. I feel terrible about my communication glitches and the mistakes I make. The burden of my own sins can become very heavy.

During my pastoral ministry, I remember being called to the bedside of an elderly man who was dying. Time and again he needed to hear that he was forgiven by God. The weight of his sin and failure crushed him during his final hours. He needed to know that Jesus really washed his sins away. It was so difficult for him to believe as he faced death.

This crushing guilt can haunt all of us. We can feel like King David did as he spoke in Psalm 51:3, *"For I know my transgressions, and my sin is always before me."* Sometimes your most difficult challenge is to live with yourself.

I hit one of my more memorable golf shots on a recent golf outing. It wasn't a par, birdie, or eagle. It was a ball that ricocheted off a fence and went through the window of a house along the golf course. At a very high speed and with a loud crash, that ball did some real damage. The owner of the house came out as I rode my golf cart toward his back yard. Fortunately, no one was hurt and he was very kind. I apologized profusely and we exchanged contact information so I could pay for the broken window. But I felt terrible. In addition to being embarrassed, I felt awful for the waste of money this round of golf would cause. Here I was trying to fund college tuition for my daughters, and I was throwing away a couple of hundred dollars on my lousy golf game. The more the day went on, the worse I felt. I was beating myself up for my inept actions. By the end of the day I had convinced myself that I was an all-time loser who should never pick up a golf club again.

That's the downward spiral of not being able to forgive yourself. You become worse and worse in your own eyes. Your failures become bigger and bigger. Pretty soon you feel as if you don't deserve to live on the planet, let alone receive any kind of favor, affection, or affirmation from anyone in your life. Your guilt grows and your personal value disappears. While my broken window wasn't all that serious, you may struggle with some devastating consequences to your actions. How can you forgive yourself? Do you even deserve it?

Of course we don't deserve it. But God doesn't operate according to what we deserve. Psalm 103 brings us a beautiful message:

> *The LORD is compassionate and gracious, slow to anger, abounding in love. He will not always accuse, nor will he harbor his anger forever; he does not treat us as our sins deserve or repay us according to our iniquities. For as high as the heavens are above the earth, so great is his love for those who fear him; as far as the east is from the west, so far has he removed our transgressions from us (vss. 8-12).*

121

This is remarkable and life-changing forgiveness. The New Testament put it this way: *"But God demonstrates his own love for us in this: While we were still sinners, Christ died for us"* (Romans 5:8). God is gracious to us as we fail, fumble, and foul everything up. He looks for failures! He lives to seek us out. As Jesus said, *"I have not come to call the righteous, but sinners"* (Matthew 9:13).

But how can you forgive yourself? It all starts the way this chapter began: with a conversation and letting go. Your own failures are the heaviest burden. You can't carry that load. Jesus invites you to give it to Him. I had to talk to God about my broken window. I told Him how lousy I felt and asked Him to carry the embarrassment and pain for me. I talked to my wife about my foul-up. I took time to think and pray. Every time I began to beat myself up, I remembered that God has a plan, He is in control, and He can even redeem my ineptitude. He can make a silk purse out of any sow's ear that I create in this world. I must trust Him with my mistakes and failures. I must watch and see what He will do with not only my best in life, but my worst.

Once you start letting go of your failures and following God where He leads you on the journey of forgiveness, you'll even begin to forgive yourself. You'll see God grow you, give you new life, and let you live in a new place—a place of second chances.

When you let go of the pain and hurt and allow God to do His job, you'll experience the miracle of forgiveness. You'll be struggling well.

Study Guide for Chapter 5:
Struggle Well with Humble Forgiveness

1. Contrast the effects of forgiveness and unforgiveness in your life and in your relationships with others.

2. Read Psalm 6:2-10. Describe the emotions expressed in this Psalm.

3. What help does the writer rely on?

4. How does this Psalm encourage and guide you when you face struggles in relationships?

5. How does prayer help you let go of your relationship wounds?

6. Read Luke 5:27-32. How did Levi demonstrate repentance?

7. Why was repentance such an important emphasis in Jesus' ministry?

8. What does repentance mean for you at this time in your life?

9. What should you forget and what should you remember when you forgive someone?

10. What makes it difficult to forgive yourself? Talk about forgiveness challenges you're having and how prayerful "letting go" can help.

Chapter Six
Struggle Well
with Genuine Gratitude

you get to, not you have to.

---

*"Why are you downcast, O my soul? Why so disturbed within me?
Put your hope in God, for I will yet praise him, my Savior and my
God." Psalm 42:11*

*"Then they cried out to the LORD in their trouble, and he
delivered them from their distress." Psalm 107:6*

Thank You

I read about Ray Nilsson the other day. He was Garrison
Keillor's father-in-law. Mr. Keillor wrote an article about him
called "Despite a cruel final hand, he gave thanks" (San Antonio
Express-News, May 15, 2010). Ray was a thankful man. In the
article, Keillor summarized Ray's life and his last days:

> Mr. Ray Nilsson died in an upstairs bedroom in my house
> early Monday morning around 2:35 a.m.

> It was cruel, the last hand that life dealt him, multiple
> myeloma, months of veering wildly between excruciating
> pain and drugged stupor, and so it was a blessing when at
> 2:35 a.m., he simply drew a long breath and then not
> another one. He was 10 days shy of his 88th birthday.

We choose comfort instead of uncertainty.

He was a gentle Swede, an orderly man, a man of powerful memory who could recall exactly how he had gone about laying the concrete steps at his cabin 30 years before and recall this in such excruciating detail that you wanted to jump out the window. He could remember the day when, as an infant, he took his first steps—he really could—and he could remember every moment of that afternoon when a beautiful young woman from Rutherford, N.J., had come knocking at the door of his parents' rooming house in Minneapolis, looking for a room for her brother, and something electric passed between them, which led to a long, loving marriage.

He made his living as an elected official, the clerk of district court, and left it with no regret to embark on a long and happy retirement, walking two miles a day, reading history, listening to Beethoven and Schubert and Bach, cutting wood, shoveling his driveway.

I suppose there is no good way to die, but Ray made the best of his. He resisted painkillers, wanting to keep his mind clear. He expressed satisfaction with his life. He showed his vast love of his four children and his wife. And throughout his misery, he said "Thank you" over and over and over. Those were the last words he said, two days before he expired.

Ray Nilsson was a thankful man. During the most difficult time in his life, as the breath of earthly existence was leaving his body, Ray's gratitude swelled to a beautiful crescendo that culminated in his final words: "Thank you."

Many Complaints

Ray didn't grow up in the age of convenience and quickness. His world was the hard to come by, do it yourself, scrimp and save, go-without-until-you-can-pay-for-it kind of existence. His way of living was slower and simpler. No, it wasn't perfect, but it was unique and beautiful.

Today, we're spoiled. Food is fast, access is instant, travel takes practically no time, purchasers can have it now, and help is just a few clicks of a phone keypad away.

Yet, we complain:

"This computer is taking forever to boot up!"

"I can't believe my flight is delayed for an hour!"

"I think I was sitting at that stoplight for five minutes!"

"What? My order isn't ready at the drive-thru window yet?"

What happened to us? How did we become such a bunch of grumblers? What do we really expect—everything to be instantaneous and totally satisfying all the time? Instead of being patient and longsuffering, instead of savoring life and living in the moment, instead of counting our blessings, we complain.

It is so easy to slip into negativity. Perhaps it goes back to mistaken expectations—a false perception of what life is really like, as we discussed in chapter two. If we blend our false notions of what life is supposed to be like with everything we see and hear all around us, the combination could be disastrous.

127

Think about it. The average American watches over 28,000 minutes of television commercials each year. Add this to the images on the internet, in magazines, and on billboards, along with all of the television, video, movie and other media content that fills our lives. These images portray what life is supposed to be like. We internalize that artificial reality. We expect it to happen. When it doesn't, when life is messier and more difficult, we become indignant, angry, frustrated, and dissatisfied. We grumble. We complain. Gratitude is drained out of our lives.

No Contentment

But it's not just the media's fault. Our natural tendency is to complain. In our broken and sinful state, we always veer away from being grateful.

> *When life is messier and more difficult, we become indignant, angry, frustrated and dissatisfied. Gratitude is drained out of our lives.*

I remember when my wife started to give our first child baths. She was so tiny, bath time was in the kitchen sink. How our little girl howled with a complaining cry! My wife was determined, however. She smiled and laughed and convinced our daughter to love her bath. It was good for her. It was a something to be grateful for.

How we howl with complaints and dissatisfaction in life! We don't want our old things anymore. We want the newest and the latest. We compare our lives to our neighbors and want their "perfect" situations. When we like something, we're not content to enjoy it. We want it. We want to possess it.

You may remember when you could only see movies in theaters. It was a big event to go to the "show." If you were fortunate, you were able to see a new movie when it was released. But once you enjoyed your big screen experience, that was it. It was over. You had your memories, but you would not see that movie again. The scenes would have to live in your imagination. The feelings of awe would have to be treasured up in your heart and mind. You and your friends could talk about it and relive it in conversation, but once it was finished playing in theaters, it was gone.

These days, it's a different story. When someone likes a movie, they say, "I want that." And they can get it. They may never watch it again, but they can own it. They can possess it. It feels good to have it. Unless we have it, we're not satisfied. Storage facilities, garages, basements, and closets are filled with things we had to have. We are not content, not satisfied, until we have more and more and more, the newest and the next thing.

It's no secret that we live in an age of addiction. Addiction is consumption. Instead of expressing satisfaction with what we have, we seek satisfaction in what we don't have. We look for contentment in the next thing—the next purchase, drink, snack, hit, or rush of excitement. We crave wholeness and think that we will find it by acquiring or consuming something out there.

Even if you live a fairly well adjusted life, free from extreme addiction or consumption, the cultural climate still has an insidious influence on you. It may show itself in a simmering spirit of dissatisfaction. Your life feels ordinary. Your spouse isn't as ideal as you'd hoped. Your home or apartment isn't the kind of place you thought you'd have. Your clothes don't seem as stylish as everyone else. Life just isn't enough. And it makes you feel inadequate, lousy, and never satisfied.

When Life Isn't What You Hoped For

Sometimes you have reasons for deep disappointment. When your life goes seriously wrong, extinguishing your hopes and dreams, how can you not become weighed down with confusion, hurt, and emptiness? How is it possible not to live in dissatisfaction?

The Biblical character Naomi would be near the top of my list as a candidate who could claim the right to complain. Naomi was from Bethlehem long before Jesus was born there. She and her husband, along with their two sons, fell on hard times as a famine ravaged their homeland. Unable to make ends meet, they moved to a foreign land where crops were growing and the promise of prosperity was stronger. While they were in this unfamiliar place, Naomi's husband died. Suddenly, Naomi was left to raise her sons alone, a defenseless woman in a strange country.

Naomi's sons grew up and each married a woman from that nation. For ten years, Naomi enjoyed life with her family, but, once again, tragedy struck. Both of her sons died. Naomi had no claim on her daughters-in-law. They were free to go back to their parents. After hearing that food was now available in her hometown, Naomi resolved to go back home—alone.

Logically, this story should have ended tragically. A woman who had no family support or protection from a man was heading for disaster in the ancient Middle East. A woman with no children suffered a critical eye from the culture and didn't fit into any social niche. Naomi faced hopelessness.

But God showed Naomi that there is always another side to the story. As Naomi said goodbye to her daughters-in-law, one of them, Ruth, spoke up: *"Don't urge me to leave you or to turn back from you. Where you go I will go, and where you stay I will stay. Your people will be my people and your God my God. Where you die I will die, and there I will be buried. May the LORD deal with me, be it ever so severely, if anything but death separates you and me" (Ruth 1:16-17).* A bright spot of love and loyalty appeared for the lonely and hurting widow. Together, Naomi and Ruth traveled back to Bethlehem.

You may know the story. God provided food and shelter for the women. He then blessed them with a kind man who fell in love with Ruth and invested his time and money to acquire the family land. This man, Boaz, became a "kinsman-redeemer." He stepped up to rescue Naomi and her family from being destitute outcasts. At the end of the book of Ruth, Boaz and Ruth gave birth to a son. Naomi's peers praised God for His gracious provision in her life: *"Praise be to the LORD, who this day has not left you without a kinsman-redeemer. May he become famous throughout Israel! He will renew your life and sustain you in your old age. For your daughter-in-law, who loves you and who is better to you than seven sons, has given him birth" (Ruth 4:14-15).*

There's always a different perspective—even to tragedy. God redeemed the heartbreak and loss of Naomi. In fact, He gave her more blessings than she realized. Naomi's grandson was named Obed. Obed, the son of redemption, became the "father" of redemption. From Obed's family line would come Jesus, the Redeemer of the world!

A New Perspective

When my family returned from a mission trip in Africa, we came home with a new perspective. If we left with any dissatisfaction, we returned with grateful hearts. I used to complain about the pothole-ridden Chicago area roads. After driving in Africa, the roads where I lived seemed luxuriously smooth. Living in a fast-moving and fashion-conscious suburb, we would sometimes complain about our wardrobes. We came home thankful to God that we were blessed with what we had. The best dressed people in the village we stayed in had one or two outfits. A good number of people had no shoes. Spoiled with overflowing resources, we could get pretty negative and feisty about minor inconveniences. We arrived home with grateful hearts for accessible medicine and health care, plentiful food, the freedom to worship Jesus, and a stable nation. Our perspectives had changed.

When I was a pastor in Minnesota, I visited the Mayo Clinic in Rochester, Minnesota regularly. Whenever I stopped there I was ministering to people with serious health issues. But during every visit, instead of hearing complaints, I heard thanksgiving. People would always say, "We thought we had it bad, but we're so grateful. Every since we've been here, we see that our problems could be so much worse." Perspectives had changed.

There is always a story behind the story. There is always a reason for gratitude. This is true not because there is always a bright side or silver lining here and now. Sometimes life is very bad and doesn't get better. But by God's grace, we always have another story. Behind every hurt, want, tragedy, failure, and loss, we've been woven into the story of salvation. We've been given a new and deeper perspective. No matter what happens here and now, we know that restoration and complete redemption have been accomplished by Jesus. One day, when we see Him face to face, everything will be okay. Even when life gets difficult and dissatisfying here and now, eternity breaks through as Jesus walks with us, encourages us with His Word, enters our lives through baptism, puts our souls back together with the gift of the Lord's Supper, and opens up access to His help in prayer. This is why the Apostle Paul could say, *"Do not be anxious about anything, but in everything, by prayer and petition, with thanksgiving, present your requests to God. And the peace of God,* which transcends all understanding, will guard your hearts and your minds in Christ Jesus" (Philippians 4:6-7). Thanksgiving can overcome anxiety because God has written a new story for each of us. He's given us a new, blood-bought, resurrection perspective.

> *Thanksgiving can overcome anxiety because God has written a new story for each of us. He's given us a new, blood-bought resurrection perspective.*

Struggle Well with Genuine Gratitude

The Apostle Paul also said, *"Be joyful always; pray continually; give thanks in all circumstances, for this is God's will for you in Christ Jesus" (1 Thessalonians 5:16-18).* God wants you to give thanks. In every situation, His desire is that you express gratitude. God must know something about struggling

133

well. The One who knows our tendency to complain and to become dissatisfied also knows the danger of grumbling and gives us the foolproof antidote to our dissatisfaction.

In 1 Corinthians 10, grumbling is listed among the serious sins that destroyed the people of Israel. Complaining and grumbling blind us to God's blessing and grace. If we're always unhappy about what we don't have, there will be no room to be thankful for what we do have. In fact, unthankfulness will crush our spirits, turn us inward, and cut us off from God and His plan for our lives. A spirit of unthankfulness will keep us from the growth that can take place as a result of adversity. Constant complaining will prevent us from seeing God's plan unfold before us.

But gratitude can change that. Thankfulness can revamp our outlooks and renew our souls.

The prophet Habakkuk asked some very difficult questions about life's unfairness and its overwhelming injustice and evil. At the end of his writing in the Old Testament, he didn't receive completely satisfying answers. But he knew God existed and was at work. Habakkuk's strengthened faith and clarified perspective led him to declare: *"Though the fig tree does not bud and there are no grapes on the vines, though the olive crop fails and the fields produce no food, though there are no sheep in the pen and no cattle in the stalls, yet I will rejoice in the LORD, I will be joyful in God my Savior" (Habakkuk 3:17-18).* If everything was fouled up and he didn't have what he hoped for, he would still be grateful.

Gratitude expressed Habakkuk's trust that there was another reality; there was more to the story. Hearty thanksgiving

134

pulled Habakkuk out of depressing negativity, led him into an attitude of hope, and conditioned his soul to make God's difference in the world.

Gratitude can do the same for you. When you're weighed down with burdens, God invites you to find what you can be thankful for. When you see all the things you wish you could have, God leads you to rejoice in what you've got. When you wonder if your life is worth anything, God sends you on a quest to give thanks for whatever you can. When struggles hit, genuine gratitude can counteract the depressing and distressing emptiness, dissatisfaction, and restlessness that come with trial. Giving thanks in all circumstances pulls you from the pit of preoccupation with self and leads you to the appreciation of what is precious and important in your life. Gratitude helps you rejoice in what is important, what is happening in the moment, and how God has walked with you throughout your life.

A friend of mine experienced the death of her husband and all the heartbreak that comes with such a difficult loss. After the funeral, she resolved not to get trapped in runaway despair and woe. Her strategy to keep going was to give thanks. Immediately, she started writing thank you lists. The first one was a twenty-six item "Thank you ABC's." In every creative way possible, she kept giving thanks. When darkness and despair loomed, she pushed its dominance away with sincere thanksgiving. She struggled well.

I remember plenty of days when I had too much trouble, not enough money, not enough time, and too many demands. When the burdens piled up and my attitude started to sour, I would head out on a long run, determined to give thanks. Sometimes I would run for ten miles and challenge myself to say thanksgiving

135

prayers the whole way. It's amazing how much you can remember to be thankful for when you work at it. My mother has an autoimmune disease called Sjögren's syndrome. Its major affect on her body is that she has no tears and very little saliva production. I remember cascading prayers of thanks that finally led me to thank God for my saliva! How often did I thank Him for that in my life?

I would return from my run with a new outlook and perspective. True, there was much to be concerned about. Yes, there was a lot I couldn't afford. Of course, I had some real challenges and troubles. But in the midst of all the struggles, I had so many reasons to give thanks. Gratitude kept me balanced. It put my life into proper perspective.

Gratitude does the same in our relationships with each other. I know a man with a crippling disability. He can't get around very easily and must use a wheelchair when he leaves his home. I remember seeing him help his wife set the table for dinner. It took him a long time and he couldn't accomplish the task perfectly, but his wife thanked him for the help. Instead of grumbling about what he couldn't do, she thanked him for what he could do.

This is a major outlook changer. If children thank parents for what they have, complaints about what they don't have will diminish. If parents affirm their kids for the good they do, negative feelings about what they don't do will fade into the background. If husbands and wives express appreciation to each other for the way they bring blessing to one another, the affirmation will crowd out complaints that crop up in a relationship. Genuine gratitude, finding what to be thankful for, expressing sincere appreciation, remembering the gifts of God in your life, will help you struggle

136

well. Giving thanks will help deliver you from the life-souring lust for more. Discovering blessings will give you hope. Genuine gratitude will make you a person people want to emulate. Your thankful heart and spirit will shine the light of our gracious Father in heaven who is the Giver of all good things.

What's Your Refrain?

An effective way to check your level of gratitude in life is to listen for your "refrain." A refrain is the part of a poem or song that is repeated over and over again. Your refrain is the recurring words, actions, and attitudes of your life. What is your refrain?

The world is full of negative and thankless refrains. These tend to be contagious. They seep into our psyches and we find ourselves repeating them—even if we know they're not really accurate. They become easy to say—a reflex response to a variety of situations.

> *The world is full of negative and thankless refrains. These tend to become contagious. They seep into our psyche and we find ourselves repeating them.*

I've noticed that negativity can infiltrate most life situations. When a person announces his upcoming marriage, someone never fails to say, "You're losing your freedom! It's time for the ball and chain!" When parents announce the birth of a baby, there is always a person who chimes in, "You're life is never going to be the same! Have fun missing out on sleep for a few years!" When children are growing up and parents are enjoying the blessing of family, how do people respond? "Just wait till they're teenagers! You won't have much fun then!"

Negativity barges in so easily. Unthankfulness tries to spoil blessings and squelch joy. It happens with school, jobs, travel, possessions, life-transitions, youth, age—everything! People can find something wrong in every situation. A refrain of complaint and criticism can dominate your life.

As a pastor I had to fight negative and critical refrains. When our church was small, people and colleagues from outside the church would drift into complaint-mode about what we couldn't do, how other churches were so successful, and how we would never amount to much. When our church was big, people would grumble about how big churches were too impersonal and that we grew because we must have been doing something to water down the message. When we were in building programs, fellow pastors would moan and groan about the cost, the mess, and all the hard work.

Negative refrains ran rampant. I decided that I would counteract these unthankful choruses. I made sure that I praised God for every season of our church's life. I spoke openly to the congregation about the wonderful season of ministry God was providing. I joined the people of the church in thanking God for the opportunity to have the messes and inconvenience of growth. Every time someone spoke negatively, I tried to lift up what we could be thankful for.

Why did I do this? It wasn't because I was so brainy. It was because God provided a new refrain in His Word. Over and over again in the Bible, we see refrains of thanksgiving and trust.

138

One such refrain is: *"Give thanks to the LORD, for he is good; his love endures forever."* This simple and beautiful phrase is found in 1 Chronicles 16:34, Psalms 106:1, 107:1, 118:1, 118:29, and 136:1. The abbreviated cry of gratitude, "His love endures forever," is repeated forty-one times in the Old Testament. Psalm 136 alone repeats the phrase twenty-six times! If you read the context of the verses, you see that this refrain counteracted the worst of life. It beat back the refrains of ingratitude, negativity and the loss of hope. It pushed away pride and drew drifting strugglers back to the Giver of all good things.

In 1 Chronicles, David composed a Psalm of thanks as the Ark of the Lord was brought back into the midst of the people. The Israelite army conquered the Philistine enemy. David's thanksgiving gave credit to God for the victory and pushed away any pride that would well up because of his new fame.

Psalm 106 is filled with repentance and the admission of failure. God's people disobeyed Him and let Him down time and time again. Instead of veering into hopelessness and despair, the writer holds onto a refrain of thanksgiving for the bountiful mercy of God. Forgiven gratitude overcame punishing guilt.

Psalm 107 recalls people who were scattered and wandering, hungry and thirsty, suffering and near death. The verses plunge us into the experience of being imprisoned in the deepest gloom and darkness. Then, life-shattering foolishness, disobedience, and trouble give way as thanksgiving for God's healing prevails. The writer takes us to the treacherous high seas that struck fear in the hearts of men and to parched deserts that dried the very life out of helpless wanderers. Seasons of oppression, calamity, and sorrow sweep into our lives, but over and over again, through every imaginable difficulty and disaster, a refrain of thanksgiving brings the relief of God's rescue and redemption: *"Let them give thanks to the LORD for his unfailing love and his wonderful deeds for men."*

Psalm 118 is bookended by the refrain of thanksgiving: *"Give thanks to the LORD, for he is good; his love endures forever."* In between these first and last verses of gratitude are crises and life-lessons, pressure from enemies and blessings from God. Through it all, negativity loses its grip as the refrain of gratitude is lifted up.

Psalm 136 recounts the wonder of creation, the history of God's people, and the closeness of God who cares deeply about our lives. Through all the ups and downs there runs a thread of thanksgiving. It is the refrain that binds life together well. It is the refrain that leads us to face any struggle and struggle well.

What is your refrain? Are you starving for times in life that are better? Do you look back and feel as if the best days of your life have passed you by? Do you feel like you're drowning in pain? Are you in agony because of injustice? Do you wonder if you've been abandoned by God?

As those feelings welled up in the struggling believers who wrote Psalm 42, a refrain of thanksgiving and trust restored their strength and hope. They cried out, *"Why are you downcast, O my soul? Why so disturbed within me? Put your hope in God, for I will yet praise him, my Savior and my God."*

This powerful refrain is voiced in verses one and five of Psalm 42. But it didn't end there. Showing how these powerful words spill over into the ebb and flow of life, the refrain bursts the barriers of one Psalm and explodes into the next. Psalm 43:5 repeats the refrain again: *"Why are you downcast, O my soul? Why so disturbed within me? Put your hope in God, for I will yet praise him, my Savior and my God."*

Suddenly, confidence replaces negativity, salvation replaces sin, and reaching with the truth replaces being mired in darkness.

What will you have as your refrain in life? There are many possibilities, but genuine gratitude puts life back into perspective and refreshes the soul. Genuine gratitude pulls you back from distant loneliness to a close and secure walk with your Savior who loves you. If you need to be convinced, take a look at Jesus.

Jesus' Final Word

Jesus lived a refrain of gratitude. During two key moments of His life, He showed that a grateful spirit helped Him to struggle well.

After Jesus' close friend Lazarus died, He went to visit Mary and Martha, Lazarus' sisters. After a powerful dialog about their faith, Jesus broke down in tears. He was moved and saddened by the grief of His dear friends. Filled with feelings of deep emotion, Jesus made His way to the tomb. Already dead four days, Lazarus' body lay behind a stone that sealed the grave. Martha was hesitant to have the stone removed. The body would be decaying already and the smell would be strong and foul. But Jesus insisted. The stone was taken away and the stench of death filled the air. Mourners wept. Gloom and sadness gripped the hearts of every person there.

In that moment, what did Jesus say? He began with gratitude: *"Jesus looked up and said, 'Father, I thank you that you have heard me'" (John 11:41).* At one of the most sad and difficult times of Jesus' life, He thanked the Father in heaven for listening. A great miracle would follow. Jesus raised Lazarus from the dead. But preceding the miracle was the thanksgiving refrain of the Son of God.

Not long afterward, Jesus found Himself living through the most difficult night of His life. It was Thursday of the week of Passover, the night Jesus would be betrayed, arrested, and beaten. He had less than twenty-four hours to live. Agonizing and painful hours awaited Him. What did Jesus do? Matthew, Mark, and Luke tell us:

> *After taking the cup, he gave thanks and said, "Take this and divide it among you. For I tell you I will not drink again of the fruit of the vine until the kingdom of God comes." And he took bread, gave thanks and broke it, and gave it to them, saying, "This is my body given for you; do this in remembrance of me" (Luke 22:17-19).*

Framing Jesus' institution of the Lord's Supper is His refrain of thanksgiving. On a dark and deadly night, Jesus gave thanks to His Father. When the pressure was on, Jesus expressed gratitude. As He wondered whether or not the Father might take this ordeal from Him, Jesus gave thanks. Knowing His disciples would abandon and betray Him, He thanked God for His blessings.

Genuine gratitude flowed from Jesus' heart, mind, and soul. His refrain of gratitude helped Him struggle well.

So Many Reasons

For Thanksgiving Day one year I wrote a song with a refrain that, I hope, captured the dynamic we face every day:

> *There are so many reasons to cry,*
> *So many reasons for tears in my eyes,*
> *But there's one thing I'll say, too,*
> *There are so many reasons to thank you.*

There are so many reasons to feel like you want more. There are so many reasons to veer into dissatisfaction. There are so many reasons to become frustrated. There are so many reasons to be sad or distracted or busy or out of sorts. There are so many reasons to struggle poorly. The world will throw all those reasons at you. But genuine gratitude can change that.

Being thankful for what you have will help you overcome unhappiness about what you don't have. Expressing gratitude to people in your life will lift people up and make a positive impact in your relationships. Giving thanks to God for the blessings He's given you will help you connect with God's presence and realize His love and care for you every day. Living with a refrain of genuine gratitude will make you a shining light of God's grace in a dark and dissatisfied world.

Ray Nilsson knew that. He showed that to his loved ones. Ray Nilsson helped show the world that genuine gratitude can soak into your struggles—even the most extreme struggles—and will lead you to do something extraordinary: to struggle well.

143

Study Guide for Chapter 6:
Struggle Well with Genuine Gratitude

1. What drains gratitude from your life?

2. What about our culture perpetuates grumbling and dissatisfaction?

3. What do you grumble about most?

4. Read 1 Thessalonians 5:16-18. Talk about how these verses challenge you, and how you might be able to follow them in your life?

5. Read Ruth 1:16-22. Naomi was having a difficult time— particularly with God. How do these verses guide you in working through your struggles with God?

6. What negative or destructive refrains easily become part of your life?

7. What God-given refrains have you learned that can replace the ungrateful ones?

8. Read Psalm 136 and Psalms 42-43. Discuss the context of the refrains in these Psalms and why you think the refrains are helpful.

9. How can these refrains be used during your struggles and during your successes?

10. What area or areas of your life need to be transformed from grumbling to gratitude?

Chapter Seven
Struggle Well
by Losing Yourself

"For it has been granted to you on behalf of Christ not only to believe on him, but also to suffer for him, since you are going through the same struggle you saw I had, and now hear that I still have." Philippians 1:29-30

"The cords of death entangled me, the anguish of the grave came upon me; I was overcome by trouble and sorrow. Then I called on the name of the LORD: 'O LORD, save me!'" Psalm 116:3-4

It's Not About Me

In 2006 Blake Mycoskie traveled to Argentina for a vacation. While visiting, he noticed two things: first, a unique type of shoe worn by Argentine farmers; second, the lack of shoes for children. Without shoes, children experienced cuts on their feet that led to infection and illness. Without shoes, children couldn't attend school. Without shoes, children were disadvantaged and in danger. Blake had an idea. Returning home with a backpack full of shoes, he started a company called "TOMS Shoes." "TOMS" isn't the name of a person. It stands for "Tomorrow's Shoes." Blake's goal was to reserve a pair of free shoes for a child in need every time a customer purchased a pair of TOMS footwear. He would then help deliver the free shoes to the children. One year after starting this venture, Blake and his team returned to Argentina to give away 10,000 shoes to children in need. The idea caught on. By the first part of 2010, TOMS Shoes had given away 600,000 pairs of shoes worldwide.

Why is there such interest in TOMS Shoes? Why have major clothing companies come alongside this little start-up venture to help support what the company calls "the one-for-one movement"? Because people want their lives to make a difference in the world.

Blake calls himself the Founder and Chief Shoe Giver of TOMS Shoes. Instead of labeling himself a CEO and plunging into a self-indulgent lifestyle, Blake spreads the word about the cause as he visits college campuses and participates in shoe giveaways in communities all around the world. The movement is a growing and unconventional approach to business. It weaves philanthropy directly into product purchase and promotion. Anyone can make a significant difference in the life of a child by buying a pair of shoes. The remarkable response shows that people want to make a profound impact in the lives of others. Jesus said, *"Is not life more important than food, and the body more important than clothes?" (Matthew 6:25)* People know there is something more. People have a deep need to live beyond the mundane, beyond the superficial, and beyond the self. But it's not easy to get to that point.

The Culture of Me

A few years ago, country singer Toby Keith wrote a song called "I Want to Talk About Me." The chorus declares:

> I wanna talk about me
> Wanna talk about I

Wanna talk about number one
Oh my me my
What I think, what I like, what I know, what I want, what I see
I like talking about you you you you, usually, but occasionally
I wanna talk about meeeeee

It's a humorous song that highlights our deep desire to matter and to make an impact. It's also a song that shows the errant pathway we take to try to meet this need. It is so easy to become all about ourselves. Me, me, me. We believe that by grabbing attention, by living a life focused on ourselves, we will get noticed. And getting noticed, we tell ourselves, means we've achieved significance.

No doubt you experience the strong pull of the culture to live a life focused on yourself. As the customer, you're always right. As an individual, you're told to look out for "number one." Products are designed to pamper you, to make you comfortable, and to insure your happiness. Services are advertised to let you know that you shouldn't be inconvenienced. You're told that you deserve the best life can give. You are entitled to nothing less than complete satisfaction. These messages are used to sell you things, but they shift your thinking away from serving others to dwelling on you, you, you.

Our culture of celebrity also tries to pull you inward. To be successful these days means that you're "known." People do almost anything to get on TV or to become the latest viral video on the internet. This quest for notoriety has eroded privacy, boundaries, propriety, and ethics. It has, in fact, fueled hurtful and criminal behavior—just so people can feel like they're noticed.

> *Instead of existing to saturate the community with the love and truth of Jesus, a local church can become preoccupied with serving itself.*

Even the Christian Church has been drawn into the "me" game. On one hand, a mentality of fame pervades the Church. Small churches and pastors who aren't well known can become driven to "make it big" by building giant buildings, starting massive programs, or by gaining worldwide recognition. If they don't write a best-selling book, compose a widely read blog, have the most friends on Facebook, or host the most popular conference, they may wonder if they really matter. On the other hand, a trend of institutional self-preservation has gripped the Church. Instead of existing to saturate the community with the love and truth of Jesus, a local church can become preoccupied with serving itself. The self-destructive focal points of staying comfortable, paying the bills, and making sure outsiders don't rock the boat can take hold in the life of the congregation. Me, me, me, distracts the people of God from their real purpose of self-sacrificial outreach.

The Culture of Mean

In the desperate attempt to grab hold of significance, people have also become mean. A mean spirit has permeated our culture. Of course, the world has never been perfect. Kindness has never oozed from the pores of all of humanity. But being mean seems to have reached a new level.

For a while, a talk show's popularity seemed directly proportional to the number of fistfights it could generate. Television news channels have moved from coolheaded discussions to shout-fests that rely on rants and insults. Television shows and movies portray "cool" people as the ones who can make the most sarcastic and disrespectful remarks. Mean is popular. Mean makes you cool. Mean gives you attention. That's what we're told.

Jesus warned us that a spirit of meanness would be prominent in the days before His return. In Matthew 24:12 He said, *"Because of the increase of wickedness, the love of most will grow cold."* Love is self-sacrificial. In 1 Corinthians 13 the Apostle Paul described love this way: *"Love is patient, love is kind. It does not envy, it does not boast, it is not proud. It is not rude, it is not self-seeking..."* That kind of love, Jesus said, would grow cold as the end of the world drew near. Meanness would prevail.

The dangerous and destructive menace of meanness is upon us. It's stylish to be mean. Parents snap at their children. Children sass their parents. Friends torment each other. Bullying has moved from the playground to cyberspace. Children have been driven to suicide because of the assault of meanness. Verbal pummeling has become commonplace as people lash out electronically. People are trying to lift themselves up by putting others down. It is a twisted epidemic in the quest for personal happiness and significance.

The Culture of Misery

But trying to find contentment and self-worth by turning inward always fails. Me, me, me, always results in misery. This misguided direction in the search for happiness always leads people down a path of hopelessness and despair. Jesus said, *"Whoever wants to save his life will lose it" (Matthew 16:25).* Being all about you will destroy you.

What is the best course of action, then, when you desperately want to find significance? What can you do when you're tired of life as usual? What pathway can you take when you feel trapped in a season of life that drains life from you?

You know that life can get that way. When our children were babies, it seemed as if we would never again get a full night's sleep. My wife and I felt like we would never be able to go to a movie or eat a meal without being interrupted. As day after day and night after night wore on, we became completely worn out by the endless routine and constant demands.

I've had jobs that seemed very shallow and one-dimensional. They weren't very fulfilling. I needed to make money. That was the grand purpose of my employment. As I struggled to make a living, it was not always easy to get up and go to work. Feelings of purposelessness did not help me with my attitude or work ethic. And when a boss was lousy or a customer was unpleasant, I wasn't motivated to excel at my tasks. Being miserable at work was a battle.

There are many other difficult seasons in life. There are times when you feel miserable. Grief can take over your existence. Betrayal can make you bitter. Depression can paralyze you.

What can you do in these situations of misery and pain? What can you do when you want more than that?

I know parents who have shoved their children aside and run away into a life of self-indulgence. The struggle was too much for them. Usually it was a father or mother who bailed out, leaving the other parent to handle the parenting load.

I've worked with people who have checked out of their jobs mentally. If their work felt meaningless and they were being hassled too much, it was time to take advantage of the system. One of my co-workers napped all day while the other people on the shift took care of business. Another got lost in personal computer pursuits, looking busy, but accomplishing nothing for the organization.

Are those the answers to misery? Should you dive further into yourself? Should you curl up in a ball and refuse to step out of the house? Should you lash out at other people? Should you retreat into addictions that give you a temporary feeling of being okay? Or is there more to life? Is there more to significance? Is there a way to struggle well in your quest to be a meaningful part of this world?

The Bigger Picture

Some of the Biblical personalities we've met in this book help answer these important questions. Joseph was a young man on a quest for significance. He wanted to be important. He wanted to be loved. He dreamed that he was being worshipped! But God showed him that his meaningful contribution in the world would not be achieved by becoming ego-driven and self-indulgent. Joseph would find significance, contentment, and happiness only after he lost himself completely. It was a crushing blow when he lost everything and was shipped to Egypt. He wasn't thrilled with his new job there. He didn't aspire to be a lead servant in Potiphar's house or to be Pharaoh's right hand man. Joseph would have rather been at home in familiar and comfortable surroundings. He would have preferred life as the favored son in his father's land. But God had a different plan. God led Joseph to swallow his pride and humbly accept a different assignment. It's interesting to note that by losing himself, Joseph was more effective in his tasks. Instead of falling in love with his job and surroundings, instead of worshipping his position and title, Joseph kept his focus on how he could serve and depend on God. Losing himself, letting go of his pride and agenda and traveling steadily on God's path, allowed Joseph to reach a lost nation with the Good News of the Savior God. Joseph became a significant leader; he made a powerful difference in the lives of others, only after he stopped focusing on himself.

Daniel got a glimpse of God's bigger picture, too. This young man in exile learned quickly that life was not all about him. Throughout his decades of captivity, Daniel lost everything except his walk with God. But in losing himself, he witnessed the remarkable work of God to transform the lives of countless numbers of people in the Babylonian and Medo-Persian Empires. Daniel could have easily wallowed in self-pity. He could have whined about the radical changes in his life. He could have become resentful and self-serving. He could have become a mean and bitter man, lashing out at his captors. But instead, Daniel struggled well by living for a greater reality than his personal comfort and desires. He lived as an instrument in the hand of God for the purpose of reaching the lost. From moment to moment and from day to day, the bigger picture of trusting God and discovering His purpose was Daniel's hope. Humble service in spite of discomfort and grief was Daniel's bigger picture path. Daniel became a person who made a difference. He became significant, not by trying to grab attention, but by losing himself to God's will and ways. The Bible expresses the principle well: *"Humble yourselves before the Lord, and he will lift you up" (James 4:10).*

> *Humble service in spite of discomfort and grief was Daniel's bigger picture path.*

Jonah had to swallow some significant pride as well—or should I say he had to get swallowed up in his pride! He started out by struggling poorly. He ran away. He tried to hide from God. He made every effort to push God's plan aside and assert his own agenda. But God wouldn't let him go. In the belly of the great fish, Jonah realized the bigger picture. He faced the fact that what really mattered was losing himself for the sake of the eternal impact of the Savior. With stinginess still lingering and God's reprimand still stinging, Jonah obeyed God's call to reach out to the wicked city of Nineveh. Jonah didn't like the result. He became angry about Nineveh's repentance. He moped and complained. But God had the last word. The final verse of the book of Jonah is a question from the lips of the Lord. God's inquiry echoes into our temptation to make life all about ourselves: *"But Nineveh has more than a hundred and twenty thousand people who cannot tell their right hand from their left, and many cattle as well. Should I not be concerned about that great city?" (Jonah 4:11)* There is a bigger picture. It is concern for others. It is reaching outside yourself.

155

Jesus is the epitome of One who lost Himself for the bigger picture of the salvation of the world. We hear the theme directly from Jesus and throughout the Bible. Jesus said, *"The Son of Man did not come to be served, but to serve, and to give his life as a ransom for many" (Matthew 20:28).* Philippians 2:5-8 underscores Jesus' ultimate sacrifice:

> *Your attitude should be the same as that of Christ Jesus: Who, being in very nature God, did not consider equality with God something to be grasped, but made himself nothing, taking the very nature of a servant, being made in human likeness. And being found in appearance as a man, he humbled himself and became obedient to death--even death on a cross!*

This is the attitude we adopt to realize true significance. This is where real joy is found. Jesus let go of everything. He lost His life so each one of us could receive the gift of new life. He gives us all we need so we can be freed from the desperate quest to fill our emptiness and prove that we're worth something. You are already worth every thing to God! The Bible says, *"How great is the love the Father has lavished on us, that we should be called children of God! And that is what we are!" (1 John 3:1)* Life is no longer about the struggle for recognition and purpose. You are treasured by God and have been given an eternal purpose.

Jesus calls us to that grand and selfless path in Mark 8:34-35: *"If anyone would come after me, he must deny himself and take up his cross and follow me. For whoever wants to save his life will lose it, but whoever loses his life for me and for the gospel will save it."*

I'll never forget a ministry mentor of mine who called pastors to this humble, ego-sacrificing, servant pathway. He reminded all of us that there was a bigger picture. Ministry was not about us. We were called to lose ourselves for the sake of God's people. By doing that we would truly gain. In his old age, this pastor would stand up at conferences and shout Jesus' words from Mark 8 to every pastor in attendance. This, he said, is the essence of what we were to be about. This is what every believer is to be about. This is true significance.

The New Testament religious power brokers worried about their own status. As Jesus increased in popularity, they said, *"If we let him go on, pretty soon everyone will be believing in him and the Romans will come and remove what little power and privilege we still have" (John 11:48 The Message).* But Jesus called people to radical self-sacrifice. He said, *"Listen carefully: Unless a grain of wheat is buried in the ground, dead to the world, it is never any more than a grain of wheat. But if it is buried, it sprouts and reproduces itself many times over. In the same way, anyone who holds on to life just as it is destroys that life. But if you let it go, reckless in your love, you'll have it forever, real and eternal" (John 12:24-25 The Message).* If you're looking for life as you struggle, you struggle well when you lose yourself.

It's not easy. It means letting go of what is most important to you. In Acts 10 and 11 Peter had to let go of the traditions that shaped his entire life. A vision from heaven showed him that what he considered unclean was not necessarily correct. Shortly after his vision, Peter visited Cornelius' house and saw the gathering of Gentiles eager to hear the Gospel. These experiences led Peter to declare: *"I now realize how true it is that God does not show*

157

favoritism but accepts men from every nation who fear him and do what is right" (Acts 10:34-35). After the Gentiles were baptized, Peter had to face his Jewish peers to explain his actions. Peter summed up the events by referencing losing himself to God's bigger picture: *"If God gave them the same gift as he gave us, who believed in the Lord Jesus Christ, who was I to think that I could oppose God?" (Acts 11:17)* Peter had to accept God's leadership and guidance even though it ran against his preconceived notions, traditions, and desires. Peter risked his comfort level, popularity, and acceptance to obey God. But by losing himself, he became a significant instrument of God to reach the outcast Gentiles.

Later in Acts 16, Paul and his ministry partners pushed to enter some key regions for mission work. Time and again they were stopped—not by enemies, but by the Holy Spirit! Paul saw key ministry needs. He wanted to share the Gospel. He was passionate about changing people's lives with the Good News. His intentions were pure. But God had a bigger plan. Acts 16:6-10 recounts the startling events:

> *Paul and his companions traveled throughout the region of Phrygia and Galatia, having been kept by the Holy Spirit from preaching the word in the province of Asia. When they came to the border of Mysia, they tried to enter Bithynia, but the Spirit of Jesus would not allow them to. So they passed by Mysia and went down to Troas. During the night Paul had a vision of a man of Macedonia standing and begging him, "Come over to Macedonia and help us." After Paul had seen the vision, we got ready at once to leave for Macedonia, concluding that God had called us to preach the gospel to them.*

158

Paul and his group could have pushed their agenda. They could have stuck with their plan. But they had to lose themselves. God had a plan. It may not have made sense to them. They may have felt very strongly about missing out on critical mission opportunities. But they had to humble themselves and follow God. There was a bigger picture. It was mysterious. It didn't come complete with all the answers. But in losing themselves and submitting to God, they made a difference that changed the world.

Your Life and the Bigger Picture

Sometimes it is so difficult to look past yourself and your situation. When deep inner hurt reaches a level of intensity you never imagined, it is so easy to believe that God has forsaken you, that He has forgotten you, and that He has no clue where you are and what you're going through. You feel small, insignificant, and unnecessary. Even worse, you feel unwanted. There have been times when I felt as if God had cast me aside. As I mentioned before, the words of Psalm 102 felt so true to me: *"For I eat ashes as my food and mingle my drink with tears because of your great wrath, for you have taken me up and thrown me aside" (vss. 9-10).* But the same writer who penned those words stepped back to see the bigger picture. In verse seventeen he declared about God, *"He will respond to the prayer of the destitute; he will not despise their plea."*

God never leaves you. He never forsakes you. You are not forgotten. You are never unnecessary. The words of Jeremiah 29:11 give the great promise of God: *"'For I know the plans I have for you,' declares the LORD, 'plans to prosper you and not to harm you, plans to give you hope and a future.'"* Each breath you take and every beat of your heart has a grand and wonderful

159

purpose in God's plan. You may not always see the difference you make, but the significant spiritual impact of your very existence can never be underestimated. God is at work in you and through you. Even when you feel useless, God is at work behind the scenes doing something remarkable with your life. One day you'll see how the eternal plan played out. But before you see that heavenly perspective, you can trust that God is faithful.

Even in your most miserable situations, there is a bigger picture. This is difficult to hear and often can't be heard until some grief and pain subside. But God can redeem even the worst that life can bring. You may have heard someone quote Romans 8:28: *"And we know that in all things God works for the good of those who love him, who have been called according to his purpose."* This verse is not just true for Joseph, Daniel, Jonah, Jesus, Peter, and Paul. It is true for you. Sometimes God uses the worst situations in your life, your broken dreams and dashed hopes, to make the most significant differences in you and through you. Are you willing to lose yourself for God's bigger picture? Are you willing to trust that God will come through when you have no control and are lying face down on the ground in humble brokenness? Your time of greatest weakness may be God's time of greatest impact.

The Puzzling Plan

All of this can be very puzzling and mysterious. Paul admitted the mystery of God in Romans 11:33-34, *"Oh, the depth of the riches of the wisdom and knowledge of God! How unsearchable his judgments, and his paths beyond tracing out! 'Who has known the mind of the Lord?'"* We can't figure God out. We cannot relate to him as a peer or equal. We can't evaluate His plan and offer some suggestions that will make it better. Instead of negotiating or fighting or trying to outsmart God, we're called to lose ourselves and submit to His plan. But in God's economy, losing yourself does not diminish you; it expands your view. Paul summed up this discovery in Philippians 3:7-8, *"But whatever was to my profit I now consider loss for the sake of Christ. What is more, I consider everything a loss compared to the surpassing greatness of knowing Christ Jesus my Lord."* Losing meant gaining. Loss meant profit. Selflessness meant a fuller self. Stepping aside meant being used for the greatest impact. It is counterintuitive. It goes against the fiber of our being. It is the opposite of what the world says. But this plan of God allows for making a true difference in the lives of others. It opens the door to genuine significance. It meets our deepest needs.

> *In God's economy, losing yourself does not diminish you; it expands your view.*

God works in mysterious ways. Who can figure Him out? When Isaiah foretold the coming Savior, he didn't use words of war or conquest. Instead, the time of the Savior would look like something we could never imagine: *"The wolf will live with the lamb, the leopard will lie down with the goat, the calf and the lion and the yearling together; and a little child will lead them" (Isaiah 11:6).* Jesus helped us understand that the counterintuitive is God's specialty. In Matthew 20:16 He said, *"So the last will be first, and the first will be last."*

Some of the most profound actions of God in history were implemented through people who were completely distant from

Him. One of the most remarkable examples is King Cyrus. In the book of Ezra we hear that Cyrus helped rebuild the temple in Jerusalem. He was instrumental in the restoration of God's people. Two hundred years before Cyrus or Persia were even known, God gave a glimpse of His mysterious plan. In Isaiah 45:13 the Lord declared: *"I will raise up Cyrus in my righteousness."* God wasn't going to use the church. He wasn't going to put together a task-force of faithful believers. He was going to use an unbelieving outsider as His chosen instrument to advance the Kingdom.

This is very challenging. It means that we're not the be-all and end-all. It means that we're not the experts. It means that God can do anything He wants to. It means that He is running the show. We're servants. We follow. We receive what he graciously gives. His way is the only way. We're called to say humbly, "Yes, sir. Anything you say." There are times we may want to be at the center of the action, but God may choose to have us sit quietly on the sidelines. There are times we may prefer to be sitting on the sidelines, but God may call us to get into the thick of His action for others. It's God's choice. It's His plan. We are called to lose ourselves and let God show us how He wants His difference made, how He wants to use us for His perfect plan.

Struggle Well by Losing Yourself

What is the best course of action to take when you yearn for significance? What pathway should you walk when you want to succeed and make a difference? What should you do when you feel dissatisfied, restless, and or purposeless? I hope this chapter has shown you that you struggle well by losing yourself. You struggle well by serving. You struggle well by living the new, self-sacrificial life Jesus has given you.

For a number of years I helped lead a weeklong camp experience for students heading into high school. The preparation for the week involved taking college-age leaders through an orientation process. These young adults would serve as counselors for small groups of the younger campers. The group of counselors–in-training consisted of the best of the best. They were talented and outgoing young men and women. There was no doubt that the hundreds of young campers who would arrive very soon would idolize this cool group of people. But the week was going to be grueling. There wouldn't be much time for socializing or fun with college friends. This was a week of giving all the attention to the kids. It was a week of service and sacrifice from sunrise to well past sunset. In order to cultivate this mindset, I asked the counselors, "What is your hope and prayer for this week?" I'll never forget the answer of one of the counselors. His name was TJ. He stood out as a particularly likely crush for the girls and a cool dude to emulate for the boys. He was chiseled, tall, and dashing. He had a killer smile, a smooth voice, and a charismatic personality. I knew he would be one of the most popular counselors, and I thought he would answer the question with a "cool-guy" type of response. Instead, he said something I'll never forget. In a humble, sincere, and self-effacing way, he said, "I'm praying that I can reach just one person for Jesus this week."

This young man could have commanded a lot of attention and reveled in all kinds of adoration throughout the week. Instead, he lost himself and pointed everyone to Jesus. He forsook the lure of popularity and asked Jesus to use him for real significance. Instead of trying to prove himself and make his mark, he served God's children. And that week, TJ was used by God to transform the lives of several young people in very significant ways. Against the push of the world to seek attention, TJ struggled well.

You may have heard of Phil Vischer. He was a chief developer of the famous Veggie Tales videos. After being kicked out of Bible College, Phil pursued his desire to make a difference for Christ in the world. Using his computer graphic arts talent and interest, he concocted videos of cartoon vegetables that told Bible stories. The idea was a smash. From 1993 to 2003, 25 million videos were sold. His company, Big Idea Productions, was in full swing. Hundreds of staffers were hired. Phil thought he would be the next Walt Disney. He *wanted* to be the next Walt Disney. His efforts started to be more about himself and his company than about God and His mission. He wanted to grow things bigger and bigger. But then the bottom dropped out. High production costs and low revenue from a major Veggie Tales motion picture hurt the company. During this time of weakness, a lawsuit drained millions from the company's resources. Lay-offs followed. Then bankruptcy. Everything was lost. Even the characters Phil created were sold. His dream had died.

As he hit bottom, Phil realized that he was worshipping the dream, not God. The dream had become his idol. He became so caught up in his personal plans and ambitions that his attentiveness to God's plan disappeared. As he struggled to grow the company, he did not struggle well. Phil reached a point of clarity about the quest for significance. He said, "The impact God has planned for us doesn't occur when we pursue impact; it happens when you pursue God" ("Dream." Presentation by Phil Vischer at the 2005 Willow Creek Promiseland Conference.).

I met a man in Africa who learned that God's ways are much greater than his own ways and that in the middle of discomfort, God still has a plan. The man's name was Hamadoum. Hamadoum grew up in a Muslim family. Because he expressed a sincere desire to know God, his parents sent him to an Islamic teacher. He and a group of children followed their Islamic teacher and learned from him. When Hamadoum was in sixth grade, his teacher told him that Allah would condemn him to hell if he continued to go to school. Hamadoum promptly dropped out. By the time he was twenty-years-old, Hamadoum could read and recite the entire Quran. He was ready to be released from his teacher, so he went back to his own village, filled with knowledge, ready to know God better.

After being back in his village for three months, Hamadoum had a dream. He saw a burning fire—a bright light—and heard a voice say, "I see that you are seeking God, but unless you change the path you are on, you will never see God." Hamadoum was puzzled and scared. He thought this dream was from Satan. When he finally drifted off to sleep again, he had the same dream. Completely unnerved, Hamadoum moved out of the house he was staying in. He thought it had an evil spirit.

But every Friday, in the wee hours of the morning, the same dream came to him with the same voice that said, "I see that you are seeking God, but unless you change the path you are on, you will never see God." Hamadoum thought he was dying! He tried to stop the dream. He chanted verses from the Quran. He visited Islamic teachers for advice. He even consulted witch doctors. Finally, one very powerful man said to him, "This light and voice are more powerful than anything I know of."

Hamadoum didn't know what to think. One Friday, after the dream came again and woke Hamadoum from his sleep, he asked the voice, "Who are you?"

The voice answered, "I am the way and the truth and the life." The voice told Hamadoum to go see a man in his village named Eli.

Eli was a Christian pastor. Hamadoum did not want to go. But because he was afraid of the voice, he did. He met Eli at his home. Hamadoum greeted Eli with the traditional tribal greetings. Then he sat before Eli, saying nothing. He looked at Eli and looked away. He shifted in his seat, stalling, afraid and unwilling to speak. Eli finally spoke up, "You Muslims search for God. But I want to say to you that Jesus alone is the way and the truth and the life."

Hamadoum was shocked. His heart raced. Those were the words of his dream! But he said nothing and left. He didn't want to hear this. This is not what he thought should happen.

But Hamadoum was desperate. He prayed to God, "Help me to find the truth that comes from you. Help me to understand what you want me to understand."

That night, Hamadoum had another dream. It was different than the dream that had been recurring for weeks. In this new dream Hamadoum received a book. On the cover of the book was written, "The book of life." In the dream, he read the book.

Two days later, after hearing that Christian evangelists were visiting the village, Hamadoum took a route through the village that would avoid any contact with them. As he walked

166

home that evening, a man approached him, handed him a book, and left without saying a word. Hamadoum looked at the cover. It said, "The book of life." He remembered his dream and began to read the book.

Hamadoum began to struggle well that day. Instead of wrestling with torment and turmoil, pride and pain, Hamadoum lost himself and gave in to God's reach into his life. He read the book he received, a French New Testament, and the living Word of new life flooded His heart, soul, and mind. Finally an answer. Finally, the truth. Hamadoum trusted His Savior, the Way and the Truth and the Life, Jesus Christ. Today, he helps translate the Scriptures into his tribal tongue and reaches out to an area of Africa populated with nearly 500,000 people who do not know Jesus. In fact, a few Christmases ago, Hamadoum helped read the account of Jesus' birth in Luke chapter 2 to the people of his village in their native language. It was the first time this happened in the history of the world.

Will you let God show you the way to true significance? Will you trust God when your life is at a low ebb? Will you serve others when you feel like pulling inside yourself and shutting out the cruel world? Will you surrender your pride and humbly obey God's leading? Will you struggle well by losing yourself?

I was in the Milwaukee airport recently. After I made my way through security, I came to the area where people were repacking their bags, putting shoes on, getting dressed, and trying to regroup. It was the typical mess we encounter these days in airports. But I noticed something different. Whoever runs the Milwaukee airport is struggling well. A big sign was placed over the post-security gathering space. It said, "Recombobulation

167

Area." I laughed out loud. Instead of ignoring the shoeless, half-dressed, unpacked passengers, the folks in Milwaukee put aside pride and admitted the predicament. With some humor, they struggled well.

How is God leading you to let go of your pride and agenda in the midst of challenge? How is He leading you to face your difficulties with a serving heart and spirit? How is God leading and strengthening you to struggle well by losing yourself?

Study Guide for Chapter 7:
Struggle Well by Losing Yourself

1. What symptoms of a "me-culture" do you notice in your day to day life?

2. Have you noticed a meaner tone in our culture? Talk about what red flags of meanness you see.

3. Read Luke 12:16-20. How does this parable relate to today's self-indulgent culture?

4. How does the parable relate to the temptations you face?

5. Read Luke 12:21. What does this verse mean for our lives on this earth?

6. Read Mark 8:34-35. What has happened in your life to show you the bigger picture of finding true significance in self-sacrifice?

7. What self-sacrifices in your life have challenged you?

8. How have you seen these sacrifices benefitting others?

9. Read Mark 10:42-45. To what areas of service is Jesus calling you these days?

10. What current struggles in your life might be eased by serving others?

Chapter Eight

Struggle Well
by Accessing Hope

---

*"My comfort in my suffering is this: Your promise preserves my
life." Psalm 119:50*

*"Not only so, but we also rejoice in our sufferings, because we
know that suffering produces perseverance; perseverance,
character; and character, hope. And hope does not disappoint
us..." Romans 5:3-5*

Facing the Impossible

In 1901, after unsuccessful summer experiments with
flying an airplane, Wilbur Wright wrote:

> When we left Kitty Hawk at the end of 1901, we doubted
> that we would ever resume our experiments. Although we
> had broken the record for distance in gliding, and
> although...our results were better than had ever before
> been attained, yet when we looked at the time and money
> which we had expended, and considered the progress
> made and the distance yet to go, we considered our
> experiments a failure. At this time I made the prediction
> that men would sometime fly, but that it would not be
> within our lifetime.

Wilbur lost hope. He felt that human flight was not in the picture anymore. In fact, his brother Orville chimed in later as he remembered those days of toil and experimentation, "Not within a thousand years would man ever fly!"

Yet, on December 17, 1903, the Wright brothers managed to fly an airplane four times, with a record distance of 852 feet in a flight that lasted fifty-nine seconds (www.eyewitnesstohistory.com /wright).

The whole venture seemed impossible in 1902. But just over 100 years later, more than four billion people around the world arrive and depart the world's airports each year. Many casually stroll onto 800,000 pound airplanes and take to the air without a second thought. What was once considered impossible is now routine.

What happened? The Wright brothers solved the problem of lift. Lift is a principle of flight directly related to the shape of the wing. When the wing is constructed correctly, it pushes air downward. This results in less pressure above the wing than there is below the wing. In other words, there is less pushing the craft down than there is lifting it up. The result is flight.

Grounded or Soaring?

Isaiah 40:31 says, *"Those who hope in the LORD will renew their strength. They will soar on wings like eagles; they will run and not grow weary, they will walk and not be faint."* The promise is that we will soar as we hope in God. But too often, doesn't it seem that there is more pushing you down than lifting you up? Doesn't soaring seem impossible?

The proliferation of the atheistic denials of God and the increasingly secularized culture tell you that you can't soar. The world says it's impossible to soar unless you have money, fame, perfect health, ideal looks, or flawless relationships. Your own heart may tell you that it's impossible to soar when the world is full of bad news and when you hurt deeply because of illness, grief, or depression.

> *As you live each day, you can feel like there is much more pushing you down than there is lifting you up.*

Struggles can make soaring seem impossible. Living with strength instead of weariness and with hope instead of despair can seem unattainable. As you live each day, you can feel like there is much more pushing you down than there is lifting you up.

The prophet Elijah felt that way. After a remarkable victory over Queen Jezebel's band of evil prophets, Elijah should have been soaring. God had come through in a remarkable way (you can read about it in 1 Kings 18:16-40). But instead, because of Jezebel's bullying rhetoric, Elijah became afraid and depressed. With all her prophets killed, the queen sent a messenger to tell the victorious prophet, *"May the gods deal with me, be it ever so severely, if by this time tomorrow I do not make your life like that of one of them"(1 Kings 19:2).*

So Elijah ran away. Traveling forty days and nights, he reached a mountain called Horeb. He crawled into a cave and went to sleep. The mighty proclaimer of God's Word was a trembling mess, grounded by Jezebel's threat. Elijah was certain that this was the end. Every fiber of his being knew that nothing could overcome this struggle. He was a goner.

But God said, "Think again." 1 Kings 19:9-10 tell us:

And the word of the LORD came to him: "What are you doing here, Elijah?" He replied, "I have been very zealous for the LORD God Almighty. The Israelites have rejected your covenant, broken down your altars, and put your prophets to death with the sword. I am the only one left, and now they are trying to kill me too."

Elijah felt hopeless, alone, and abandoned. But God replied:

"Go back the way you came, and go to the Desert of Damascus. When you get there, anoint Hazael king over Aram. Also, anoint Jehu son of Nimshi king over Israel, and anoint Elisha son of Shaphat from Abel Meholah to succeed you as prophet. Jehu will put to death any who escape the sword of Hazael, and Elisha will put to death any who escape the sword of Jehu. Yet I reserve seven thousand in Israel--all whose knees have not bowed down to Baal and all whose mouths have not kissed him" (vss. 15-18).

God gave Elijah lift. God let Elijah know that he wasn't alone. He could take heart because there were 7000 other faithful followers of the Lord. God would also provide new leadership, newly anointed kings to help defeat the enemy. Elijah wouldn't have to fight this battle himself. Best of all, God would provide a successor for Elijah. A new prophet, Elisha, would provide the help downtrodden Elijah needed. God was giving Elijah a powerful and grace-filled message: in spite of how everything appeared, there was more lifting Elijah up than there was pushing him down.

The word for "succeed" in the phrase "succeed you as prophet" literally means "underneath." Elijah was given a helper to get underneath his sagging spirit, to lighten the load, and to carry him during his struggle. Elisha would provide encouragement, help, and strength. He would be a good influence—God's influence—as the voices of destruction and negativity came Elijah's way. God provided lift to help Elijah soar again.

That's what God does. Isaiah 46:3-4 gives the good news of God's tender and encouraging help throughout struggles:

> *"Listen to me, O house of Jacob, all you who remain of the house of Israel, you whom I have upheld since you were conceived, and have carried since your birth. Even to your old age and gray hairs I am he, I am he who will sustain you. I have made you and I will carry you; I will sustain you and I will rescue you."*

God carries you. He promises to make sure there is less pushing you down than there is lifting you up. In Jesus, He got underneath you and carried the greatest weight that pushes you down. He carried your sin. Isaiah 53:4-5 speaks of Jesus' saving work,

> *Surely he took up our infirmities and carried our sorrows, yet we considered him stricken by God, smitten by him, and afflicted. But he was pierced for our transgressions,*

175

he was crushed for our iniquities; the punishment that brought us peace was upon him, and by his wounds we are healed.

Removing the burden that condemns you, shouldering the destructive weight of your sin, Jesus gives you lift. Even as struggles increase and the weight of life pushes you down, your Savior continues to provide help and hope. That's the way God works. Life is full of clutter and junk. There is so much that can make you feel lousy. The spiritual battle rages and Satan is trying to demoralize and discourage you. But God is constantly working to make sure there is more lifting you up than there is pushing you down. Sometimes God steps in with obvious assistance, bold encouragement that sits you up straight and makes you take notice of His presence and grace. At other times God acts in subtle and quiet ways—similar to the still, small, whispering voice He used to encourage Elijah. Either way, God's goal is to continue to provide you with solid, certain, and dependable hope.

The Invasion of Hope

A servant of the prophet Elisha desperately needed a dose of hope in 2 Kings 6. The angry and frustrated King of Aram sent his army to surround the city where Elisha was staying. Elisha had been thwarting the king's efforts to conquer Israel. By night, a massive army with horses and chariots encircled the city of Dothan, ready to capture the prophet. Early the next morning, Elisha's servant saw the threatening forces. He asked Elisha, *"Oh, my lord, what shall we do?"* What Elisha did next goes down in history as one of the ultimate hope-accessing moments:

> *"Don't be afraid,"* the prophet answered. *"Those who are with us are more than those who are with them."* And

Elisha prayed, "O LORD, open his eyes so he may see."
Then the LORD opened the servant's eyes, and he looked
and saw the hills full of horses and chariots of fire all
around Elisha (2 Kings 6:15-17).

God opened the servant's eyes to see the mighty and protecting armies of God. There was more to the story, much more than met the eye. What appeared to be the weight of the world, what looked like the crushing and grounding forces of impossibility, was really an opportunity for Elisha and his servant to see the hope-giving power of the Almighty God.

God invades our world with hope. As the relentless forces of the world try to drag you down, God is always present to break in with blessings that lift you up. In chapter four I mentioned Daniel's visions. God invaded Daniel's hopeless situation with vivid and compelling communication. Whenever Daniel started to get depressed and wonder if God was with him, God made sure Daniel heard from Him directly. Every time it appeared that Daniel had too much pushing him down, God counterbalanced the burdens with a vision that lifted him up.

Jesus received this helpful invasion of hope, too. God the Father provided the counterbalance of encouragement and help whenever Jesus hit the wall of hopelessness. After Jesus battled the temptations of the devil in the wilderness, Matthew 4:11 tells us, *"Then the devil left him, and angels came and attended him."* Jesus needed help and relief to lift Him up. The same toll of intense struggle dragged Jesus down in the Garden of Gethsemane. In the middle of His agonizing time of prayer before His arrest and death, Jesus received no help from His weary disciples. But God invaded the dark and draining Garden with hope: *"An angel from*

177

heaven appeared to him and strengthened him" (Luke 22:43). God provided lift for His beloved Son. Even at Jesus' baptism, as He ventured out into His new and challenging ministry, God brought hope. The Father spoke up and said, *"This is my Son, whom I love; with him I am well pleased" (Matthew 3:17).* Jesus went forward confidently. About three years later it was time for Jesus to head to Jerusalem. On the mount of transfiguration, as Moses and Elijah spoke with Jesus about His crucifixion and death, God spoke up again, *"This is my Son, whom I have chosen; listen to him" (Luke 9:35).* Heading to the struggle of all struggles, Jesus was given lift, the approving and supportive words of His Father in heaven.

> *Jesus rebuked, revealed, restored, and recalibrated His precious people. When they felt as if they were going to crash, His Word of new life allowed them to soar on wings like eagles.*

The Christian Church was invaded with hope as Jesus gave the Revelation vision to the Apostle John. God's people were persecuted and felt powerless. They were being assaulted by Roman paganism, Jewish prejudice, and their own internal problems. Many believers thought the battle was being lost. They were giving up hope. They were being pushed down under the weight of worry and suffering. Would the Church fold? Was their faith useless? As some strayed and others struggled, Jesus spoke up. He encouraged His people: *"Be faithful, even to the point of death, and I will give you the crown of life" (Revelation 2:10).* Jesus rebuked, revealed, restored, and recalibrated His precious people. When they felt as if they were going to crash, His Word of new life allowed them to soar on wings like eagles. Hope invaded utter hopelessness.

This is a basic principle of the Christian faith. Too often, however, we forget it. We forget that struggle and pain are normal in this sin-broken world and in our sin-corrupted lives. As you read in chapter two, our expectations can become inaccurate. We can start to believe that life should be ideal all the time, that we should feel great at every moment. We can fall into the trap of thinking that chaos, hurt, injustice, and suffering are abnormal intrusions into an ideal world. But this is totally untrue. The world and our lives are saturated with the hopelessness of sin, decay, and death. On our own, we're helpless. Left to ourselves, we can only conjure up the imaginary and temporary sedatives of philosophies, religions, and ideologies. Under our own power, we try to exert control or we try to mask the pain of suffering. But eventually, all of it fails.

What we really need is the invasion of hope. And that is what God accomplished. John 1:14 gives the good news: *"The Word became flesh and made his dwelling among us. We have seen his glory, the glory of the One and Only, who came from the Father, full of grace and truth."* Jesus broke into our world and lived among us. Jesus' beautiful words in John 3:16 bring us God's remarkable, miraculous, and gracious invasion of hope: *"For God so loved the world that he gave his one and only Son, that whoever believes in him shall not perish but have eternal life."* God gave us His only Son to be our Savior. Human beings never imagined such a plan. We think about how we can solve struggles by ourselves. We develop ways to make ourselves feel better as struggles rage. But a Savior? Real help? A genuine solution?

179

That's what God provided. A Savior armed with hope invaded our world held hostage by hopelessness. Because of Him, there is always less pushing us down than there is lifting us up. Because of Jesus, we have hope. Because of His work, we soar.

The Imbalance

A big question for your life is: What are you accessing? Are you tapping into more that pushes you down than lifts you up? There's plenty out there to push you down. You may even gravitate toward it. You work too many hours. You schedule too many activities. You eat too much. You drink too much. You spend too much money. You get saturated with bad news because the television is on all the time. You establish no boundaries for texting or phone calls. You listen to gossip. You hang around people who are negative influences. Soon life is out of balance. You're stressed, frustrated, distracted, in trouble, and out of control. You feel like your life is collapsing. You feel hopeless.

Unfortunately, struggles can make you feel like accessing more trouble. When life gets difficult, it is tempting to fill the emptiness with temporary and destructive fixes. A momentary "high" that helps you forget your problems for a little while becomes a habit that takes you captive and ruins your life. Denial and running away make you feel like you have freedom, but only send you running into deeper darkness and pain. Self-destructive thoughts or actions give you the illusion that your anger will make things happen the way they're supposed to, but you end up hurting yourself and others in a deep and lasting way. All of these actions throw your life into an even greater imbalance. The real answer is so close, but you keep spiraling deeper and deeper into the morass of all that pushes you down. The Wright brothers had to change the shape of the wing to achieve lift. You need the shape of your life changed.

Sometimes that simply means making a few small adjustments that tip the scales back into balance. It means finding what lifts you up and accessing it regularly. Too often we feel as if the only way out of hopelessness is a big solution, a major life-change, a complete and radical revamping of your entire existence. Out with the problems and in with perfect balance and happiness! But this is unrealistic. This world is not paradise. Struggles will always exist. What you need is lift—more lifting you up than is pushing you down. The downward forces will always be present this side of heaven, but balancing them out can change everything.

St. Paul referred to this careful life-balance. In Philippians 4:12-13 he said, *"I know what it is to be in need, and I know what it is to have plenty. I have learned the secret of being content in any and every situation, whether well fed or hungry, whether living in plenty or in want. I can do everything through him who gives me strength."* Paul had plenty pushing him down, but Jesus brought balance to his life. Through his Savior, Paul was strengthened.

Paul also mentioned the see-saw battle of life in this world as he commented in 2 Corinthians 4:8-9: "W*e are hard pressed on every side, but not crushed; perplexed, but not in despair; persecuted, but not abandoned; struck down, but not destroyed."* Two realities existed in his life. What was the secret of hanging on to hope even when life's struggles raged? He said in verse ten, *"We always carry around in our body the death of Jesus, so that the life of Jesus may also be revealed in our body."* The life of Jesus gave him lift.

I know a woman who is a vibrant person. She is a mom of two energetic young boys. But she has Multiple Sclerosis. She is in a wheelchair now. The disease has been more aggressive over the past few years and has been taking a greater toll. She has a more difficult time doing what she needs to do as a mom. She faces the financial struggles brought about because of her illness. Her self-esteem takes hit after hit. She can't do what other people can do. In many ways she is crushed. On the other hand, I received an e-mail from her recently letting me know that the Lord has led her into a vibrant prayer ministry. She believes that this is God's plan and mission for her. She is overflowing with excitement. What is going on? Balance. In the middle of deep and challenging struggle, she is accessing hope. Yes, she has to deal with very real despair. But God is also bringing her joy.

Remember, this is what God does. He invades our hopelessness with gracious and surprising hope. He provides purpose when we feel purposeless. He brings strength and resolve when we feel weak and worn out. If you're looking for a distinctive element of life in Jesus, this is it. Without Jesus, the scales of life are out of balance. On your own, you are dominated by the prevailing struggles of the day. With Jesus you're given something new. Paul urged believers to this balance in Philippians 4:5-8, *"Whatever is true, whatever is noble, whatever is right, whatever is pure, whatever is lovely, whatever is admirable—if anything is excellent or praiseworthy—think about such things."* Let God strike the balance. Struggle well by accessing hope.

Struggle Well by Accessing Hope in Others

How do you access hope?

First, you don't go it alone. Galatians 6:2 says, *"Carry each other's burdens, and in this way you will fulfill the law of Christ."* The word "carry" is the same word used for a mother carrying a baby during her pregnancy. That kind of carrying means a lot more than toting a cell phone around. It means that our very survival depends on each other. We're not together on this earth to have shallow relationships. We're not brought together as God's people to simply greet each other on Sunday mornings. We're called to bring God's help and life-renewing perspective to each other. A lifeline of hope exists in each other.

Paul emphasized that carrying each other's burdens fulfills the "law of Christ." The apostle may have been referring to Jesus' command to love each other (John 15:12, 17). Taking each other's burdens seriously and helping each other in a Christ-like way would bring full completion to this new command of Jesus (John 13:34).

But in this world of busy schedules and full social calendars, how can you find someone to help bear your burdens? In our culture of fragmented families, individualistic attitudes, and rampant loneliness, how can you not go it alone? When you hardly have time to get enough sleep, when will you be able to develop relationships that bring encouragement and help to your life?

Too often you can be led to think that relationships with fellow believers have to be in the form of friendships that dominate your life. You envision eating every meal together, hanging out after work and on weekends, and attending small group meetings and serving opportunities every week. The prospect of adding all of that to your schedule can be completely overwhelming. Is it possible to fit relationships like that into real life?

183

Frequently the church tells you that you need to find quality relationships with others in a small group program or in another ministry set up by the church. These can be very good places to meet other people and develop friendships, but a hazard of this programmatic approach can be that you start to equate meaningful Christian relationships with another activity to sign up for or another item to put on the calendar. Relationships can become artificial, awkward, and unattainable. Even worse, I believe the devil can twist this approach into a paralysis that isolates us and keeps us from receiving needed doses of hope from others. Instead of taking on another activity, we do nothing.

Who can help carry your burdens? The place to start is your family. Family counts. It is the first place where genuine, deep, and meaningful relationships are established. It is the starting point for spiritual nurture and serious interaction about what really matters in life. It's where you're supposed to be able to find a confidant, an advisor, and a friend. God designed family relationships to imitate the unconditional and self-sacrificial love seen in Jesus. In The Message paraphrase of Ephesians 5, God's intention for marriage and relationships is articulated so well. What is the purpose of a husband? *"Everything he does and says is designed to bring the best out of [his wife]."* We're put together in relationships to help make each other better. Family is where that starts.

I'm dismayed when people are directed to get involved in a variety of activities that serve God, but aren't directed to start that self-sacrificial service at home. It's worrisome when God's people are urged to use their spiritual gifts in many ways around the church and community, but are not directed to make the most of their gifts in service to their families. How unfortunate it is when couples are led to believe that friendship with their husband or wife isn't enough for a relationship of Christian accountability and growth. The people who know you the best, who care about you the most, who can speak to you with honest accuracy, and who are easily accessible are your family members. These are the people who can balance the negative assault of life in this world with the hope of Jesus. If you want to access the hope of your Savior, family is a good place to start.

Unfortunately, not everyone is able to find a resource for God's hope in their families. Your family may be broken or off track. You may not have any family members in your life. Even if you do, you may prefer the input of someone outside the family for certain issues. Sometimes a man needs to speak with a man. There are times when a woman needs to seek advice from a woman. A young person may need a peer to talk to. That's where friendships come in.

Finding friends is not always easy. As I mentioned before, people's lives are full and busy. Understanding how friendship works can be very challenging. The book of Proverbs helps us by providing wisdom about friendship. In Proverbs 17:17 God affirms the value of family and friends during times of struggle: *"A friend loves at all times, and a brother is born for adversity."* Proverbs 18:24 emphasizes that the number of people you call friend is not important; the quality of your relationship is what matters: *"A man of many companions may come to ruin, but there is a friend who sticks closer than a brother."* Proverbs 27:6 says that sometimes friends are in your life to speak the hard truth: *"Wounds from a friend can be trusted, but an enemy multiplies kisses" (Proverbs 27:6).* Proverbs 27:10 tells us that friends may be the most practical source of help during times of crisis: *"Do not forsake your friend and the friend of your father, and do not go to your brother's house when disaster strikes you-- better a neighbor nearby than a brother far away" (Proverbs 27:10).*

Sometimes having a friend means walking through life together. You spend time with each other. You talk frequently. You live close by. At other times having a friend may mean experiencing "friendship moments." God may bring a person into your life for a special reason, for a one-time encounter, or for a short period of time. A wise woman told me: "There are people God puts in your life for a reason, a season, or a lifetime." God may decide to bring you hope by having someone befriend you at a time in your life when you need it most. You may never see that person again, but God may have provided that friendship experience to lift you up in your time of need. Even if you haven't found a "best friend for life," friendship moments show you that God is working in your life. He is helping you to struggle well. He is showing you that He cares about you, that you're not forgotten, and that, through His people, He is bringing you much needed encouragement and hope.

Accessing hope by not going it alone may also mean talking with someone who has been trained to help you walk through challenges. Finding a professional counselor can be an important part of struggling well. A counselor's objectivity can open your eyes to your real needs and to accurate perspectives. A counselor's knowledge can prepare you for what's ahead and alert you to pitfalls along the way. There are some issues too big for family and friends. There are some hurts too great to process casually. A counselor who can bring expertise as well as God's wisdom and insight can be a wonderful source of balance to help you soar.

Struggle Well by Accessing Hope in God

God does not want you to try to make it through life alone. He provides people in your life as resources of His hope. He also steps into your life personally. God invades your life with hope in a powerful and personal way.

In our Western culture, people intellectualize God. He becomes all about knowledge, logic, and what the mind can comprehend. He becomes a set of definitions and descriptions. He is characterized as advanced, college level, text book material—outside the grasp of the common human being.

It is true that God is transcendent and incomprehensible. We will never be able to fully understand Him whose ways are higher than our ways (Isaiah 55:9). But it is also true that God came down to us. He walked with Adam and Eve in the Garden of Eden. He gave specific directions and promises to Abraham. He recruited Moses to rescue His people from miserable slavery. He stayed with His beloved people in a pillar of cloud and fire. He was present in the tabernacle and temple. He became flesh and made His dwelling among us in Jesus. His name is Immanuel—God with us. Yes, God is very big, but He is also small enough to speak our name and look us in the eyes. He is not just a thought; He is real and present. He is not just in the past; He is with us here and now.

Hope in God, the balance you need in this broken world and for your own struggling heart, is as close as the gift of baptism.

187

When the crowd heard about their hopeless plight from Peter in Acts chapter 2, they were cut to the heart and responded, *"What shall we do?"* Peter replied, *"Repent and be baptized, every one of you, in the name of Jesus Christ for the forgiveness of your sins. And you will receive the gift of the Holy Spirit. The promise is for you and your children and for all who are far off--for all whom the Lord our God will call" (Acts 2:37-39).* Peter didn't tell the group to study. He didn't declare that God was too far away and too big for their small and insignificant lives. He let them know that if they sought God's help, God would give them miraculous gifts: forgiveness of sins and the presence of the Holy Spirit. Their lives would be reshaped. They would soar with hope.

In baptism God pours His Spirit and grace into your life. He cleans you up and keeps the junk from cluttering your heart and soul. Baptism is a simple but mysterious gift. It is an understandable act that transcends knowledge. God is at work in baptism. We falter in weakness and confusion. We get tripped up by temptation and distraction. But the Holy Spirit's active work in baptism brings the certainty of God's help and hope from outside ourselves—beyond our own capabilities to reason and act. Through baptism God steps into your life to give you hope that does not depend on your fragile grip on God. Baptism connects you with God and gives you a firm foundation for struggling well.

God also meets you in the gift of Communion or the Lord's Supper. The book of Matthew tells us:

> *While they were eating, Jesus took bread, gave thanks and broke it, and gave it to his disciples, saying, "Take and eat; this is my body." Then he took the cup, gave thanks and offered it to them, saying, "Drink from it, all of you.*

This is my blood of the covenant, which is poured out for many for the forgiveness of sins. I tell you, I will not drink of this fruit of the vine from now on until that day when I drink it anew with you in my Father's kingdom" (Matthew 26:26-29).

The Gospels of Mark and Luke, as well as Paul's account in 1 Corinthians, tell us about the gift of this miraculous meal. As Jesus prepared His disciples for His death, resurrection, and ascension, He gave a gift that would insure His continued presence with them. In the eating and drinking of the bread and wine, Jesus would be present to forgive and renew. Paul commented on this enduring and miraculous presence of Jesus in 1 Corinthians 10:16, *"Is not the cup of thanksgiving for which we give thanks a participation in the blood of Christ? And is not the bread that we break a participation in the body of Christ?"* In a miraculous way, using the common elements of bread and wine—items that were connected with Passover deliverance, Jesus would continue to meet us personally for our strength and forgiveness. Allowing us to do more than simply think about Jesus during His physical absence, this mysterious participation provided real access to the risen and victorious Jesus Christ. Hope would continue to invade our lives through the precious gift of the Communion meal. When the world empties us out, we can gather to be filled with the presence of Jesus. We can access real, active, and living hope in this miraculous encounter with our Savior.

Another access point for hope from God is His living Word. The Bible is no ordinary book. Hebrews 4:12 says: *"The word of God is living and active. Sharper than any double-edged sword, it penetrates even to dividing soul and spirit, joints and*

189

marrow; it judges the thoughts and attitudes of the heart." The Word of God reaches into your life. It does not only engage the intellect. It grasps hold of your very soul. Regular reading and hearing of the Word of God balances your life with His input, His clarity, His guidance, and His life-renewing consolation.

Whenever I read through the book of Isaiah, the promises of help and hope bring me new energy and a new perspective. Something changes in me when I encounter God's precious words:

> *"So do not fear, for I am with you; do not be dismayed, for I am your God. I will strengthen you and help you; I will uphold you with my righteous right hand" (Isaiah 41:10).*

> *"'Do not be afraid, O worm Jacob, O little Israel, for I myself will help you,' declares the LORD, your Redeemer, the Holy One of Israel" (Isaiah 41:14).*

> *"But now, this is what the LORD says-- he who created you, O Jacob, he who formed you, O Israel: 'Fear not, for I have redeemed you; I have summoned you by name; you are mine'" (Isaiah 43:1).*

> *"Forget the former things; do not dwell on the past. See, I am doing a new thing! Now it springs up; do you not perceive it? I am making a way in the desert and streams in the wasteland" (Isaiah 43:18).*

The list can go on and on. Even as I struggle with deep pain, the precious Word of God brings me the sweetness of God's abiding strength and presence. I may not feel very happy about what is happening in life, but, somehow, I am content. I'm okay. God's Word brings me real hope.

These are gifts from God to cherish. These are gifts that allow you to access hope in God. In the swirl of activity that life brings; as negative and distracting messages cascade over your life; you are invited to access these conduits of hope. You are called to flood your life with God's resources. Ephesians 5:26 says that Jesus' death for you fills your life with something new. His sacrifice cleanses you *"by the washing with water through the word."* When you access what God provides, you will experience a difference in your life. You will struggle well. Isaiah summed it up perfectly:

> *Do you not know? Have you not heard? The LORD is the everlasting God, the Creator of the ends of the earth. He will not grow tired or weary, and his understanding no one can fathom. He gives strength to the weary and increases the power of the weak. Even youths grow tired and weary, and young men stumble and fall; but those who hope in the LORD will renew their strength. They will soar on wings like eagles; they will run and not grow weary, they will walk and not be faint (Isaiah 40:28-31).*

By accessing hope in God, you will soar!

Struggle Well

What about your life? How will you struggle? Will you struggle poorly? Will you slip into destructive actions, harbor angry attitudes, and speak careless words? Will you plunge into selfishness, veer into hopelessness, or lose yourself in isolation's darkness?

Or, will you struggle well?

A few years ago, my nephew was fishing off the dock of my father-in-law's cottage in northern Michigan. With every cast, he was waiting for the big catch, the lunker, the dream fish. He wanted to catch a tiger muskie, the fish of all fishes in the lake, the big cahuna, the top of the food chain. It's "the fish of 10,000 casts." My eleven-year-old nephew wanted one.

After a hopeful toss of the lure into the lake, he felt a tug. It was probably another tangle in seaweed, he thought. He reeled in his line and felt something pull hard. This was no seaweed. This was a fish! He kept reeling it in. There was even more resistance. This was the big one! As he pulled, he called for grandpa. Grandpa scrambled onto the dock and peered into the crystal clear water. At the exact same time, both fisherman saw what was on the end of the line. It was a tiger muskie—over forty inches long! Grandpa told my nephew to increase the drag on his line. My nephew fought the fish and brought him closer to the dock. That's when grandpa remembered that he forgot the net in the cottage! Grandpa ran to get the net, but time was wasting. A nine-year-old neighbor boy was with my nephew and sensed that the moment of victory was about to escape them all. He sprung into action. This fourth grade kid jumped into the lake! He chased the fish down and lifted it out of the water! He hauled it over to the dock and flopped it onto the wooden structure. The fish was shocked. It had never heard of these fishing rules! It fought back, and with a mighty flip of its fins it splashed back into the water. The nine-year-old boy wouldn't be denied. As my nephew held onto his fishing pole and watched with wide-eyed amazement, his buddy went back into the lake. He grabbed the fish again and threw it onto the dock. This time he leapt up on the dock and LAID on top of the fish! My nephew told me, "Uncle Mike, he wrestled the fish to the ground!"

After the struggle, the photos, and the celebration, the excited and weary fishermen released the behemoth back into the lake. Who would have thought such a fishing adventure could have happened? Who would have imagined that this delightful surprise awaited them?

I wonder if you're on the dock of your life today, casting, hoping, wondering if God is going to come through for you. I wonder if you're looking at your ordinary life and thinking that God can't do anything with it, that your struggles are going to define you, control you, and do you in. But God's Word says in 1 Corinthians 2:9, *"No eye has seen, no ear has heard, no mind has conceived what God has prepared for those who love him."* Yes, you will face struggles. Some will be more difficult than words could ever describe. But God has an adventure of His grace and help planned for you that is beyond expectation. He is faithful. He is close to you. He will help you through.

My prayer is that this book has shown you a new way to meet suffering. As you face challenges, pain, and storms, I pray that what is written here will equip you to struggle in a way that is good, faithful, godly, and edifying—in a way that shows the world the difference Jesus makes.

It is true: there are storms rolling in. This side of heaven, suffering lies ahead. You may feel like struggling poorly. But I pray that you, my friend, will struggle well.

Study Guide for Chapter 8:
Struggle Well by Accessing Hope

1. What pushes you down most and keeps you from soaring at this time in your life?

2. Recall and share when God gave you "lift" during a time of struggle.

3. Read John 3:13-17. In what ways does God's "invasion of hope" give you hope?

4. What practices and habits tend to drain life from you?

5. What changes can you make to alter this trend?

6. Read Galatians 6:2. Mention one or two people who help you bear your burdens. How do they bring hope to your life?

7. What changes can you make to help develop the relationships you have?

8. How have you experienced God's hope through the gifts of Baptism, Communion, and God's Word?

9. This book has contrasted struggling poorly and struggling well. What have you learned about the way you handle struggles?

10. What new insights have you gained that will help you struggle well?

About the Author

Michael Newman has served in ministry for over 20 years and continues to be active in writing, preaching, and teaching. At this time in his life he is thankful to be involved in developing missional communities in Texas. Married to his wife Cindy since 1983, they have been blessed with two wonderful daughters.

Check out these books written by Michael W. Newman:

REVELATION
What the Last Book of the Bible Really Means

SATAN'S LIES
Overcoming the Devil's Attempts to Stunt Your Spiritual Growth

STEPS FORWARD
The New Adventures of Ernest Thorpe

HARRISON TOWN
Discovering God's Grace in Bears, Prayers and County Fairs

For information and to purchase books, go to
www.mnewman.org.

Books are also available at Amazon.com or through your local Barnes and Noble bookseller.

5951881R0

Made in the USA
Charleston, SC
25 August 2010